W9-DIS-044

AN AGE OF VOYAGES, 1350–1600

BONNIE G. SMITH
GENERAL EDITOR

AN AGE OF VOYAGES, 1350–1600

Merry E. Wiesner-Hanks

For Kai and Tyr

OXFORD
UNIVERSITY PRESS

Oxford University Press, Inc., publishes works that further Oxford University's objective of excellence in research, scholarship, and education.

Oxford New York
Auckland Cape Town Dar es Salaam Hong Kong Karachi
Kuala Lumpur Madrid Melbourne Mexico City Nairobi
New Delhi Shanghai Taipei Toronto

With offices in
Argentina Austria Brazil Chile Czech Republic France Greece
Guatemala Hungary Italy Japan Poland Portugal Singapore
South Korea Switzerland Thailand Turkey Ukraine Vietnam

Published by Oxford University Press, Inc.
198 Madison Avenue, New York, New York 10016
www.oup.com

Design: Stephanie Blumenthal and Alexis Siroc
Cover design and logo: Nora Wertz

Library of Congress Cataloging-in-Publication Data
Wiesner-Hanks, Merry E.
An age of voyages, 1350–1600 / Merry E. Wiesner-Hanks.
p. cm. — (Medieval & early modern world)
Summary: This book provides coverage of the political, cultural, and social history of the world from 1350 to 1600. Contact among regions of the world expanded through trade networks, enabling a transferal of knowledge and culture among societies. With a strong focus on the Renaissance, Reformation, and Ming China, the text comes from ordinary people, travelers, bureaucrats, children, housewives, poets, and religious thinkers.
ISBN-13: 978-0-19-517672-8 — 978-0-19-522264-7 (Calif. ed.) — 978-0-19-522157-2 (set)
ISBN-10: 0-19-517672-3 — 0-19-522264-4 (Calif. ed.) — 0-19-522157-5 (set)
1. History, Modern—16th century. 2. Middle Ages—History. I. Title. II. Medieval and early modern world.
D228.W53 2005
909'.5—dc22
2004021178

1 3 5 7 9 8 6 4 2

Printed in the United States of America on acid-free paper

On the cover: This gold model ship was meant to be used as a table ornament. Artisans crafted it during the 16th-century reign of Charles V, and it is thought to represent one of his ships.
Frontispiece: Portuguese merchants arrive in Japan in this scene painted on a folding screen by a Japanese artist in the early 17th century.

BONNIE G. SMITH
GENERAL EDITOR

DIANE L. BROOKS, Ed.D.
EDUCATION CONSULTANT

The European World, 400–1450
Barbara A. Hanawalt

The African and Middle Eastern World, 600–1500
Randall L. Pouwels

The Asian World, 600–1500
Roger V. Des Forges and John S. Major

An Age of Empires, 1200–1750
Marjorie Wall Bingham

An Age of Voyages, 1350–1600
Merry E. Wiesner-Hanks

An Age of Science and Revolutions, 1600–1800
Toby E. Huff

The Medieval and Early Modern World: Primary Sources & Reference Volume
Donald R. Kelley and Bonnie G. Smith

CONTENTS

A “ marks a primary source—a piece of writing that speaks to us from the past.

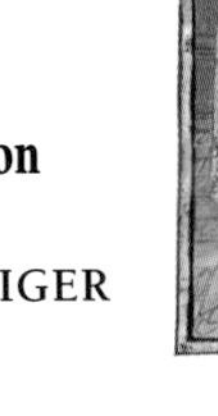

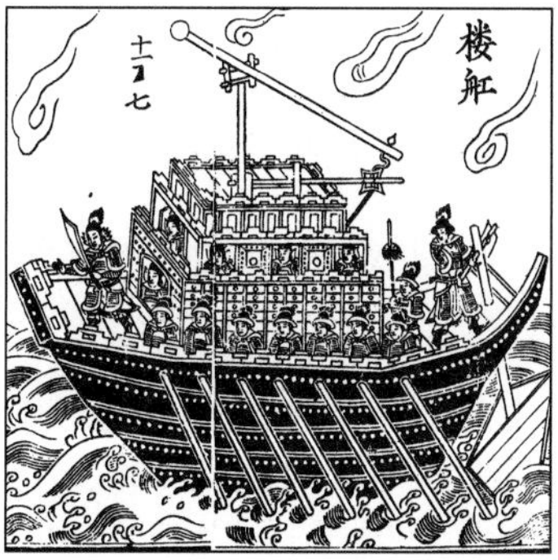
楼舡

CAST OF CHARACTERS

Afonso I (ah-FAHN-soh), ruled 1506–43 • king of Kongo

Akbar (AK-bahr), ruled 1556–1605 • Mughal emperor and religious reformer

Askia (AHS-kee-ah) "**the Great**" **Muhammad** (moh-HAH-med) **Turé** (TOO-ray), about 1441–1538 • ruler of Songhay Empire

Atahualpa (ah-tah-WAHL-pah), 1500?–1533 • Inca leader killed during Pizarro's conquest

Babur (BAH-bur), 1483–1530 • founder of the Mughal Empire

Boccaccio (boh-KAH-chee-oh), **Giovanni** (joh-VAHN-nee), about 1313–75 • Italian author of poems and stories, best known for *The Decameron*

Cabot, John (born Giovanni Caboto), about 1450–about 1498 • Genoese sea captain who headed the first English expedition to North America

Cabral (kuh-BRAHL), **Pedro Alvares** (AHL-vuh-res), about 1467–about 1528 • Portuguese adventurer who first landed in what is now Brazil

Calvin, John, 1509–1564 • French Protestant religious reformer

Cervantes (sehr-VAHN-tehs), Miguel de (mee-GEHL deh), 1547–1616 • Spanish author and playwright whose best-known work is *Don Quixote*

Charles V, ruled 1519–56 • German emperor and (as Charles I) king of Spain

Columbus, Christopher, 1451–1506 • Italian explorer, first European since the Vikings to cross the Atlantic

Cortés (kohr-TEHZ), **Hernán** (ehr-NAHN), 1485–1547 • Spanish explorer and conqueror of the Aztec Empire

Da Gama (duh GAH-muh), **Vasco** (VAHSH-koh), about 1469–1524 • Portuguese captain who first reached India by sailing around Africa

Dante (DAHN-tay) **Alighieri** (ah-lee-GYEH-ree), 1265–1321 • Italian poet

Dias (DEE-as), **Bartolomeu** (bahr-TAHL-oh-mew), about 1450–1500 • Portuguese captain who first rounded the southern tip of Africa

Elizabeth I, 1533–1603 • Protestant queen of England

Erasmus (eh-RAHS-mus), Desiderius (deh-seh-DEHR-ee-us), 1466–1536 • Dutch humanist, scholar, and author

Fang (fahng) **Xiaoru** (shyau-ROO), 1357–1402 • Chinese scholar-official, advisor to the emperor

Ferdinand of Aragon, 1452–1516 • king of Spain

Gutenberg (GOO-ten-burg), **Johan** (YO-hahn), 1400–1468 • German goldsmith, inventor of the printing press

Henry VII, 1457–1509 • king of England, grandfather of Elizabeth I

Henry VIII, 1491–1547 • king who made England Protestant, father of Elizabeth I

Henry "the Navigator," 1394–1460 • prince of Portugal who supported voyages of exploration and trade

Hongwu, 1328–98 • founder of the Ming dynasty in China, began life as **Zhu** (ju) **Yuanzhang** (ywen-JANG)

Isabella of Castile, 1451–1504 • queen of Spain

Julius II, 1443–1513• powerful Renaissance pope and patron of Michelangelo

Leonardo (lee-uh-NAHR-doh) **da Vinci** (duh VIHN-chee), 1452–1519 • Italian Renaissance artist, engineer, and inventor

Loyola (loy-OH-lah), **Ignatius** (ig-NAY-shus), 1491–1556 • Spanish Catholic religious reformer, founder of the Jesuits

Luther, Martin, 1483–1546 • German religious reformer who began the Protestant Reformation

Machiavelli (MAH-kee-uh-VEHL-lee), **Niccolò** (nee-coh-LOW), 1469–1527 • government official and writer from Florence, author of *The Prince*

Magellan (muh-JEHL-uhn), **Ferdinand,** about 1480–1521 • Portuguese sea captain who commanded the first expedition to sail around the world, though he was killed along the way

Medici (MEHD-ih-chee), **Lorenzo de'** (law-REN-dzow day), 1449–92 • ruler of Florence

Michelangelo (MY-kuhl-AN-juh-loh) **Buonarotti** (bwah-nah-RAH-tee), 1475–1564 • Italian Renaissance artist, poet, and architect

Moctezuma (mok-te-ZOO-mah) II, about 1480–1520 • Aztec emperor

Nanak Devi Ji (nah-nahk DEH-vee JEE), Shri Guru, 1469–1538 • founder of Sikh religion

Petrarch (PEE-trahrk), **Francesco** (fran-CHESS-koh), 1304–74 • Italian scholar, humanist, and poet

Philip II, 1527–98 • Catholic king of Spain, sent the Spanish Armada against the English fleet

Pigafetta (pig-ah-FEH-tah), **Antonio,** about 1490–1535 • Italian log-keeper on Magellan's voyage

Pizarro (pih-ZAHR-roh), **Francisco,** about 1478–1541 • Spanish adventurer who conquered the Inca Empire

Polo, Marco, about 1253–1324 • Venetian merchant who traveled to China during the reign of Khublai Khan

Ricci (REE-chee), **Matteo** (mah-TAY-oh), 1552–1610 • Jesuit scholar and missionary to China

Selim "the Grim," ruled 1512–20 • Ottoman sultan, effective military leader

Shakespeare, William, 1564–1616 • English playwright and poet

Sinan (SEE-nahn), **Mimar** (MEE-mahr), 1489–1588 • chief architect for the Ottoman sultans

Suleyman (SOO-lay-mahn) the Magnificent, 1494–1566 • Ottoman sultan

Sunni Ali Ber, 1430–93 • founder of the Songhay Empire

Tang (tahng) **Xianzu** (shyen-ZOO), 1550–1616 • Chinese playwright, author of *The Peony Pavilion*

Teresa of Avila (AH-vee-lah), 1515–82 • Spanish Catholic religious reformer

Tyndale (TIHN-duhl), **William,** 1494–1536 • English religious reformer and translator of the Bible

Vespucci (veh-SPOO-chee), **Amerigo** (ah-MEHR-ee-goh), 1454–1512 • Italian entrepreneur and explorer whose name was given to the Americas

Wang (wahng) **Yangming** (yahng-MING), 1472–1529 • neo-Confucian scholar

Wu Ch'eng-en (wu cheng-en), about 1500–1582 • Chinese scholar-official, author of *The Journey to the West*

Yongle (yong-leh), ruled 1403–24 • Ming emperor, sent naval expeditions to Indian Ocean

Zheng (jehng) **He** (heh), 1371–1433• Chinese admiral who headed naval expeditions to Indian Ocean

AN AGE OF VOYAGES, 1350—1600

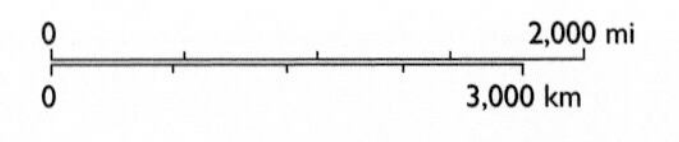

SOME PRONUNCIATIONS

Ahmedabad (ahkh-MEH-dah-bahd)

Beijing (bay-jing)

Cairo (KY-ro)

Cuzco (KOOZ-ko)

Gao (gaow)

Granada (gruh-NAH-duh)

Guangzhou (gwahng-jo)

Hangzhou (hahng-jo)

Jenne (JEH-neh)

Khanbalik (kahn-bah-LEEK)

Kilwa (KIL-way)

Mbanza Kongo (BAHN-za KON-go)

Medina (meh-DEE-nuh)

Mogadishu (mo-gah-DEE-shoo)

Nanjing (nahn-jing)

Ormuz (or-MOOZ)

Satgaon (SAHT-gah-ahn)

Tenochtitlan (teh-NOHCH-tit-LAHN)

Tunis (TOO-nis)

INTRODUCTION

The 14th century brought calamity and crisis to much of Eurasia and northern Africa. A plague killed millions of people from China in the east to Iceland in the west, while warfare and peasant rebellions disrupted society.

The late 14th century, however, also saw the beginning of political changes, an increase in trade, and developments in art and literature that radically transformed the world. In Europe, merchants in Italian cities brought luxurious goods from Asia to Europe and became extremely wealthy. They used their riches to support the flowering of art and literature that became known as the Renaissance. During this time, artists and writers looked to the classical past of Greece and Rome for inspiration, and then tried to improve on the ancient works of art. The new technology of the printing press with movable metal type speeded up communication and helped spread knowledge. And later, it also furthered the cause of religious reform and the creation of powerful kingdoms and empires.

A carving on the base of the official city scale of Nuremberg, Germany, depicts a skeleton dressed in merchant's clothes and holding a huge scale, with weights on one side and a bundle of merchandise on the other. Trade brought great wealth to merchants—two of whom flank the scale—but the skeleton was to remind them that they were still mortal and should not forget religion.

In China, a poor boy whose parents had been killed in the plague established the Ming (or "brilliant') dynasty, bringing political stability, population growth, and economic expansion. In the same way that Europeans looked to the past to create new styles in painting and poetry, Ming scholars emphasized the importance of classical teachings, especially those of the philosopher Confucius. Ming artists combined classical models and new techniques in their paintings.

Beginning in the 15th century, rulers in many parts of the world used well-equipped armies, efficient tax collectors, and capable officials to build up their own power and the power of the territories they ruled. Cities, especially those that were capitals of growing states, became metropolises, with sturdy walls, beautiful buildings, and rapidly expanding populations.

Reformers in many parts of the world challenged religious institutions that had existed for centuries. In Europe, Martin Luther confronted the Catholic Church, ushering in the Protestant and Catholic Reformations. In India, Nanak Devi Ji created Sikhism, and the Mughal emperor Akbar sought to create a state where followers of all religions could live peaceably together.

Long-distance voyages by Italian, Indian, Malay, and Arab sailors and merchants linked the Mediterranean Sea, Indian Ocean, and South China Sea by the 14th century. In the 15th century, ventures by the Chinese and then by the Portuguese widened this trading network further. Spanish, Portuguese, and English voyages in the 16th century brought the Atlantic and Pacific into this network, as spices, silver, and other goods were traded globally. Useful plants and animals spread from one area to another, but so did devastating diseases. Much of the population of Central and South America died, shaping the history of the colonies established there by the Spanish and Portuguese. The mining and processing of precious metals and the production of new crops, especially sugar, encouraged the expansion of the slave trade.

Men and women in many parts of the globe lived in a world that was far more connected in 1600 than it had been in 1350. People of great power and those of more limited means came to live their lives differently because of this expanding web of shared knowledge and trade.

Two ship's compasses from the 16th century come from very far-apart places—Italy and China—yet they are very much alike. Compasses helped sailors and navigators find their position at sea and made them more willing to sail long distances out of sight of land.

CHAPTER 1

DISEASE AND DISASTER
THE DREADFUL 14TH CENTURY

The year 1348 was a terrible year in Europe, Asia, and North Africa. An extremely contagious disease with a very high death rate spread from southwestern China all the way to Venice, Paris, and Constantinople in Europe, Tunis in North Africa, Khanbalik in China, and Damascus and Mecca in the Near East. In areas where it struck, the plague killed perhaps one-third of the population in the first wave of infection, and it kept coming back regularly during the next 300 years. In some places, including certain regions of China and certain cities of Europe, it may have killed more than two-thirds of the population. In some monasteries and villages where people lived tightly packed together, every single person died. In many areas, the people were already weakened

English and French soldiers fight on horseback at the Battle of Crécy during the Hundred Years' War. Foot soldiers and mounted knights used bows and arrows and cannons, but also fought in close hand-to-hand combat with heavy swords and long pikes.

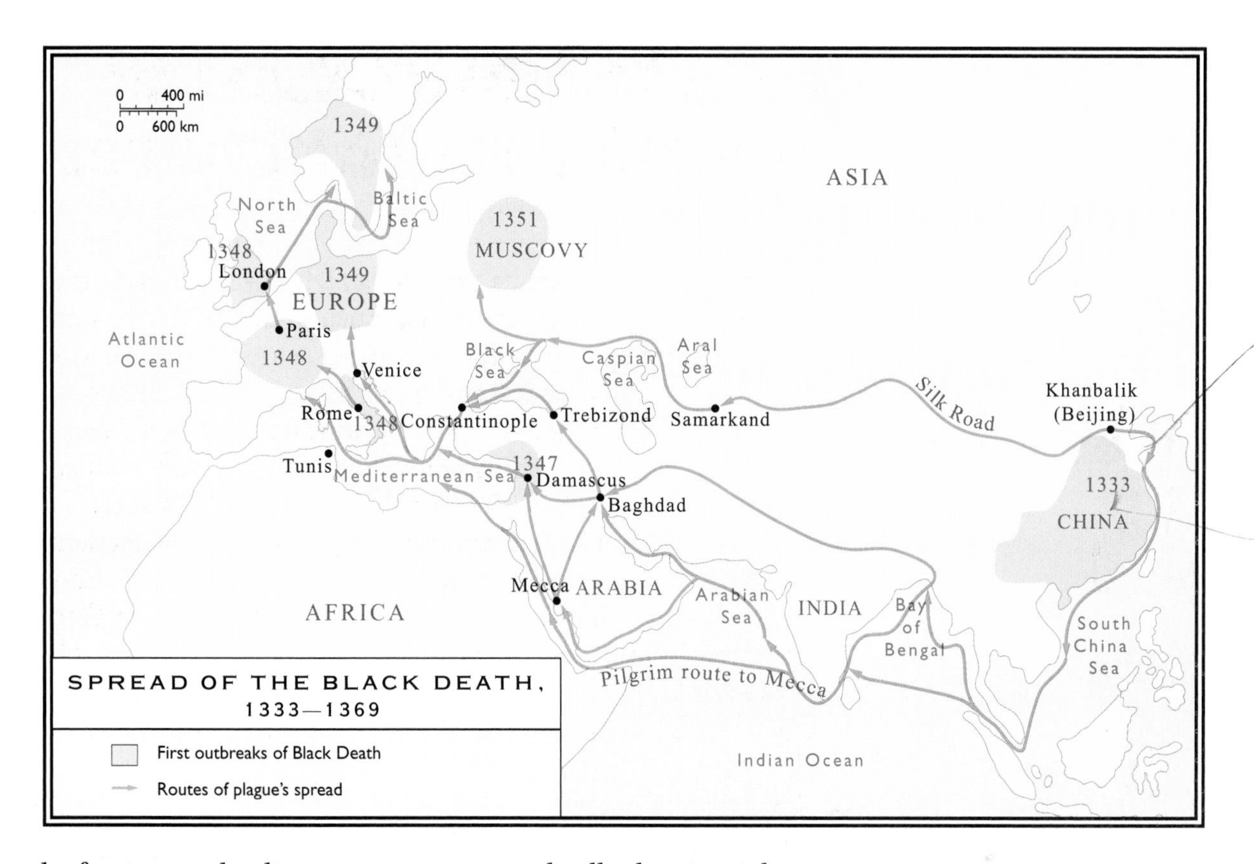

SPREAD OF THE BLACK DEATH, 1333—1369

by famine, so the disease was even more deadly than it might have been. "The year 1348 left us lonely," wrote the Italian scholar and poet Francesco Petrarch in a letter, grieving over his many friends who had died, "the life we lead is a dream, and I wish I could have woken before this."

Everywhere the plague spread, it caused changes. In 1348, England and France had been fighting for about ten years in a war that had started over who would be the next French king and who would control certain parts of France. In a blinding shower of arrows at the battle of Crécy in northern France in 1346, English archers had defeated the French cavalry and foot soldiers. Smoke from cannons—probably the first use of gunpowder in a European battle—created further confusion, and the English swooped in and butchered many of the defeated French soldiers. This battle was an early bout in a war that dragged on for another century. It was eventually called the Hundred Years' War, though it actually lasted even longer, from 1337 to 1453. The war devastated the French countryside; crops were stolen, villages were burned, and people and animals were killed.

The plague added to the misery caused by war. Adults in the prime of their working lives died along with children and older people, leaving fewer people to raise crops and do other types of jobs. The plague also left fewer people to pay taxes, which had gone up dramatically to pay for the war. The higher taxes and the destruction caused by the war led French peasants to revolt against their landlords, many of whom were nobles who did not have to pay taxes. Angry crowds attacked the noble landlords' castles and houses, burning them down, sometimes with their inhabitants in them. The nobles were terrified at first, but they united against the peasants and hired trained, well-equipped soldiers to massacre groups of peasants armed only with hoes and bread knives.

While French peasants were rebelling against their landlords, Chinese peasants were doing the same thing. China was ruled by the Mongols, people from the flat plains of central Asia who had originally been nomads, following their herds from place to place in search of pasture. In the 1100s and 1200s, the Mongols had created a vast empire under the leadership of the warrior Genghis Khan and his

A caravan travels across central Asia; camels loaded with merchandise trot in front and heavily armed guards bring up the rear. The Mongol Empire made trade along the "Silk Roads" of Asia more secure, but merchants still hired guards to protect their valuable cargo.

grandson Khublai Khan. The Mongol Empire was the largest empire the world has ever seen, stretching from Moscow (in Russia) and Baghdad (in modern-day Iraq) in the west to the Sea of Japan in the east. Mongol leaders encouraged foreign merchants to trade across their territory, allowing them to travel and send goods safely from eastern China to western Europe and back. Unfortunately these well-traveled trade routes also served as highways for the fast and easy spreading of disease.

The dramatic loss of population as the plague spread into southern and eastern China forced those who survived to work harder and longer. Landlords demanded more work from the peasants who lived on their land, which led the peasants to revolt, or to leave their villages and become bandits. The Mongol rulers could not control what was happening. In 1368, rebels captured their capital city, Khanbalik (modern-day Beijing), and the Mongols left China. Zhu Yuanzhang, the leader of the rebels, came from a poor peasant family, but he called the dynasty, or hereditary line of rulers that he founded the Ming, which means brilliant.

In eastern Europe, western Asia, and northern Africa, the plague weakened many of the existing governments, and allowed new conquerors to expand their territories. John VI, the ruler of the Byzantine Empire (the eastern half of the Roman Empire, with its capital in Constantinople, in modern-day Turkey), lost his youngest son to the plague. Just a few years later he gave up his throne and retreated to a monastery, writing in a history of the city in the 1370s, "no words could express the nature of the disease." The Ottoman Turks, a nomadic people from western Asia, gradually took over more and more of the deteriorating Byzantine Empire.

So incurable was the evil, that neither any regularity of life, nor any bodily strength could resist it. Strong and weak bodies were similarly carried away, and those best cared for died in the same manner as the poor.

—Byzantine emperor John VI, whose son died in the plague in Constantinople in 1347, in his *History*, 1370s

FLEAS, RATS, AND CATAPULTED CORPSES

Why were the effects of the plague so dramatic and devastating? To answer this question we have to know something about the disease itself, and how diseases operate. Most historians think the plague that killed so many people in the 14th century was the bubonic plague, a disease that normally

Death rides a pale horse through scenes of well-dressed people, leaving bodies and mourners behind. The bubonic plague struck rich and poor alike, including sophisticated nobles and powerful religious officials.

afflicts rats. In a cycle that sounds disgusting, fleas living on the infected rats drink their blood, the bacteria that cause the plague multiply in the flea's gut, and the flea passes them on to the next rat it bites by throwing up into the bite. Usually the disease is limited to rats and other rodents, but at certain times in history the fleas jumped from their rodent hosts to humans and other animals and infected them. This is exactly what happened in the middle of the 1300s.

Humans and rats have lived closely together since people first started gathering and storing crops, which provided easy eating for rats. Rats often carry various diseases, including the plague, and in some areas these diseases become endemic, meaning always present, in the human population. When a disease is endemic, people get sick and some die, but those who don't die build up resistance to the disease, so they do not get sick during the next outbreak. The next generation is made up of children of people who survived, so they are a bit more resistant to the disease than their parents, and so on over generations. In this way,

Europeans built up resistance, or immunity, to smallpox over many centuries, and Africans built up resistance to malaria. People still got very ill from these diseases, but they did not die in great numbers.

This may have been the case with bubonic plague in the 14th century in southwestern China. Either the plague was endemic to the population, or it jumped from rats to humans for some unknown reason. In either case, it would probably have remained a small-scale local outbreak had the Mongols not created a large empire and made it safer and easier to trade across the huge continent of Asia. Plague-infested rats accompanied Mongol armies and merchant caravans carrying silk, spices, and gold. Then they stowed away on ships, carrying the disease to populations that had little or no immunity. The plague came into densely packed cities, where, as the Italian merchant Gabriele de Mussi said in a 1348 history of the plague, "we scattered the poison from our lips" and the disease passed directly from person to person. Mussi also reported that Mongol armies besieging the city of Kaffa on the shores of the Black Sea catapulted plague-infected corpses over the walls to infect those inside. The city's residents dumped the corpses into the sea as fast as they could, but not before they became infected, and ships from Kaffa took the disease to Italy.

Carried by rats and people, the plague became an epidemic, spreading quickly and killing millions. The effects of the plague were so devastating that this first outbreak in the 1330s and 1340s is often termed a pandemic, meaning a very widespread epidemic. (The outbreak of influenza in 1918–19, which killed from 40 to 100 million people all over the world in less than a year, was also a pandemic.)

The plague had dreadful effects on the body. Reports from all over Europe, Asia, and

City residents bury the plain coffins of plague victims. The first outbreak in a city often killed so many people that families could not arrange for proper funerals, and city officials wanted the corpses buried as quickly as possible to minimize the spread of the disease.

Brother Abandoned Brother

GIOVANNI BOCCACCIO, THE DECAMERON, 1351

Giovanni Boccaccio, the son of an Italian merchant, became a scholar and professional writer. His masterpiece was The Decameron, *a collection of 100 stories told by a group of friends to each other over a 10-day period. (The word "Decameron" is based on the Greek words for 10 days.) The friends have fled the city of Florence to escape the outbreak of the plague in 1348, and in the introduction to this work, Boccaccio vividly describes the effects of the plague on the city.*

Death strangles a victim of the plague in this illustration from a Czech manuscript. Dark swellings in the armpits were common symptoms of the disease.

Against this pestilence no human wisdom or foresight was of any avail... not only did talking to or being around the sick bring infection and a common death, but also touching the clothes of the sick or anything touched or used by them seemed to communicate this very disease to the person involved.... This disaster had struck such fear into the hearts of men and women that brother abandoned brother, uncle abandoned nephew, sister left brother, and very often wife abandoned husband, and—even worse, almost unbelievable—fathers and mothers neglected to tend and care for their children as if they were not their own... so many, many people died in the city both day and night that it was incredible just to hear this described, not to mention seeing it! ... Moreover, the dead were honored with no tears or candles or funeral mourners.... So many corpses would arrive in front of a church every day and at every hour that the amount of holy ground for burials was certainly insufficient for the ancient custom of giving every body its individual place; when all the graves were full, huge trenches were dug in all of the cemeteries of the churches and into them the new arrivals were dumped by the hundreds; and they were packed in there with dirt, one on top of another, like a ship's cargo, until the trench was filled.... Oh, how many great palaces, beautiful homes, and noble dwellings, once filled with families, gentlemen, and ladies, were now emptied, down to the last servant!

North Africa give the same picture. People who were infected developed headaches, nausea, and swellings in their neck, groin, and armpits that were called buboes, the origin of the word "bubonic." Dark blotches from internal bleeding appeared on the victims' skin, which may be the origin of the term "Black Death," often used for the 14th-century outbreak of this disease. The infected person became feverish and delirious, and began to spit up blood. Once this happened, death came quickly. "In three days," reported Mussi, "whole families... were buried in one common grave." About one-third of the people who got the plague through fleabites were able to survive, but almost no one lived who got it directly through human contact.

POISONED AIR, POISONED WELLS, OR POISONED SOULS?

How did people react to this terrible disease? As we do with new illnesses today, such as AIDS (acquired immunodeficiency syndrome), people sought answers for why the plague was happening and ways to combat or prevent it. Medical doctors observed that crowded cities had high death rates, especially when the weather was warm and moist. We understand that these conditions make it easier for germs, viruses, and bacteria to grow and spread, but 14th-century people, including merchants such as Mussi and professionally trained doctors, thought in terms of "poisons" in the air rather than germs.

We say that the first cause of this pestilence was the conjunction of the planets Mars and Jupiter... which gave rise to excess heat and moisture on the earth... and corrupts the air... which, when breathed in, corrupts the life force.

—Report of the University of Paris medical faculty, October 1348

As the Arabic historian, philosopher, and statesman Ibn Khaldun commented, "the principal reason for the plague . . . is the corruption of the air through too large and dense a population." This "corrupted air" came from swamps, unburied animals or corpses, too much rain, the position of planets or stars, or perhaps other causes. These poisons, it was believed, caused illness, which doctors in Europe, North Africa, and the Near East thought of as an imbalance in the fluids of the body, especially too much blood. Doctors frequently prescribed bloodletting, that is, taking blood from the body by applying leeches or making small cuts in veins, as a standard treatment.

In China, doctors also thought about the body in terms of flow and balance. In healthy bodies, the life force, called qi or chi, flowed freely around the body, maintaining a balance between two complementary forces, yin and yang. Yin and yang were related to many pairs of opposites, including male and female, dark and light, and action and stillness. Treatments for the plague and other illnesses, including acupuncture and medicines, worked to restore the free flow of qi and the yin/yang balance.

If the plague came from poisoned air, people reasoned, then strong-smelling herbs or other substances, such as rosemary, juniper, or sulfur, held in front of the nose or burned as incense, might stop it. Perhaps loud sounds such as ringing church bells or firing the newly invented cannon might help. Medicines made from plants that were bumpy or that oozed liquid might work, keeping the more dangerous swellings and oozings of the plague away. Because the

These metal pomanders were designed to carry strong-smelling spices and herbs that people hoped would ward off the plague. Poor people made do with cloth bags of spices or with oranges studded with cloves.

ى	ف	ا	ش
302	3	79	11
78	8	302	3
4	301	9	8

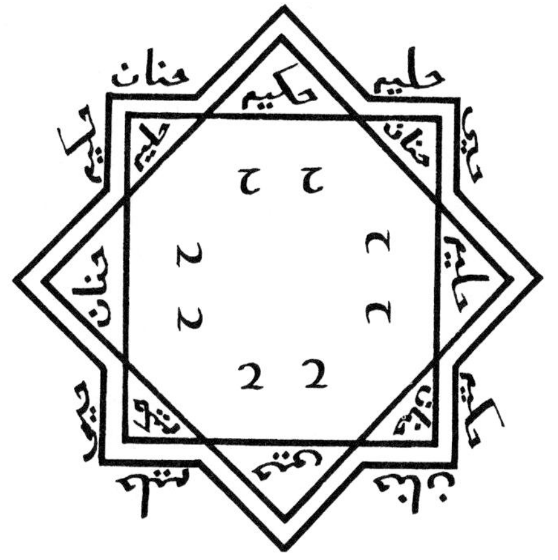

Arabic cryptograms—combinations of numbers, letters, or symbols—were believed to protect against the plague. The letters were often the first letters of words in prayers or religious sayings, and the numbers were based on ideas about certain numbers being lucky or unlucky. Carved on necklaces or written on slips of paper, cryptograms helped to give people a sense of order when faced with the randomness with which the plague seemed to strike.

plague seemed to strike randomly, perhaps wearing jewelry decorated with random number and letter combinations, or drinking water in which the ink used to write these magical combinations had been dissolved, would help.

It was clear that the disease passed from person to person, so wealthier people often fled cities to the countryside, though sometimes this simply spread the plague faster. Some uninfected cities also tried shutting their gates to prevent plague-ridden people and animals from coming in, which worked in a few cities. They also walled sick people up in their houses, isolating them from those who were still healthy.

Along with looking for medical causes and cures, people also searched for people to blame. The Christian rulers of many cities in Europe with Jewish residents required all Jews to live in a certain area of town separate from Christians. (In some parts of Europe, such as England and France, Jews were completely prohibited.) Rumors spread that Jews were spreading the plague by poisoning wells in Christian parts of town, and Christian mobs tortured and killed thousands of Jews, often by very gruesome means. Jacob von Königshofen, a Christian chronicler, reported in a city history written in the late 14th century that "Jews were burnt all the way from the Mediterranean into Germany." In his hometown of Strasbourg, on the Rhine River in what is now eastern France, "they burnt the Jews on a wooden platform in their cemetery... about 2,000 of

The procession was joined by the entire population of the town, men and women, small and large, all weeping and seeking the favor of God... and God lightened their affliction, for the number of deaths in a single day did not reach two thousand.

—Muslim geographer and traveler Ibn Battuta, whose mother died of the plague, describing reactions to the plague in Damascus in *Travels in Asia and Africa*, 1348 them" and "their wealth was divided" among the crowd that was watching. These actions did not keep the plague away, and a few months later 16,000 people died in the city. And Jews got the plague, too. "The father is left, sad and aching," said a poem inscribed on the gravestone of a 15-year-old Jewish boy in the city of Toledo in Spain.

Many people thought the plague was the result of something bad within themselves. God must be punishing them for terrible sins, they thought, so that the best remedies were religious ones: asking for forgiveness, prayer, trust in God, going on pilgrimages to holy places, making donations to churches, and trying to live better lives. Artists created, and people bought, paintings and woodcuts with images of sin and death—skeletons dancing or leading people off to an unknown fate—hoping these might ward off the plague.

In Muslim areas, religious leaders urged people to be virtuous in the face of death: give to the poor, reconcile with

Flagellants—people who whipped themselves hoping to make up for the sins that they thought brought on the plague—traveled from town to town. Officials sometimes worried that flagellants would provoke violence and riots, and ordered groups of them to disband when they grew too large.

your enemies, free your slaves, say a proper good-bye to your friends and family, and meet death the way people being martyred for their religious beliefs would. In Europe, some groups recommended more extreme demonstrations of guilt and repentance, beating themselves and marching from town to town urging others to join them. These groups, called flagellants, whipped up hysteria against Jews and often grew into unruly mobs.

Over the long run, those who survived had things a bit better. With fewer mouths to feed, each person got more and better food and clothing. Peasant farms became slightly larger. Those who worked for wages knew that because there were fewer workers, employers should pay higher wages. When employers instead tried to freeze wages and lengthen working hours, workers in many towns and cities in Europe, including Florence, Italy; Seville, Spain; and Lübeck, Germany, revolted. Like the peasant revolts, workers' revolts were brutally put down by professional soldiers, but smaller mob actions, such as boycotting or destroying the shop of an especially harsh employer, continued on and off for decades.

Both in the countryside and in the cities, people also responded to the drop in population by experimenting with more efficient ways of doing things. They tried new crops that took fewer people to plant and harvest, or switched to raising cattle, sheep, or horses, because these required even less labor than crops. They used new tools and more machinery, especially windmills and water mills for grinding grain or sawing wood. In Italy, Korea, and other areas, merchant-investors started making cloth on a larger scale, hiring many workers and reducing the cost of producing wool and cotton cloth. They then sold this cloth along the same trade routes that had carried the plague, and also searched for new markets and cheaper ways of transporting the things they were buying and selling. That search would lead to the sea, for even a small ship could carry far more than an entire camel caravan could. Ships carried the plague, but they also carried the possibility of fabulous wealth.

CHAPTER 2

RENAISSANCE MEN AND RENAISSANCE MONEY

LEARNING AND ART IN ITALY AND BEYOND

What's the best-known painting in the world? Many people would choose the *Mona Lisa* by Leonardo da Vinci, a portrait of the young wife of a rich merchant from the Italian city of Florence. The painting is small, and shows a calm young woman in a dark dress with her hands folded across one another. It's not very different from many other portraits, except for her mysterious smile, which has intrigued people for more than five hundred years. That smile shows deep insight into the complexities of human nature, one of the many things that interested the man who painted her.

Leonardo da Vinci painted the Mona Lisa *in about 1504. Her exact identity is unknown, which contributes to the mystery surrounding her smile. Computer analysis suggests to some people that she might even be a self-portrait.*

Leonardo (who is always known by his first name) wanted to reproduce things exactly as the eye saw them, and he drew everything he saw around him, including executed criminals hanging on gallows as well as lovely women and the beauties of nature. He used these drawings as the basis for his paintings, and also as a tool of scientific investigation. He drew plans for hundreds of inventions, many of which, such as the helicopter, tank, machine gun, and parachute, would only become reality centuries later. Because he had such a huge range of interests and abilities, he is often called the first "Renaissance man," a phrase we still use for a multitalented individual.

Leonardo was born in the middle of the 15th century in the small town of Vinci, near the growing city of Florence in northern Italy, where he went as a teenager to train as an artist. For several centuries, merchants in Florence, and other nearby cities, had been growing wealthy from buying and selling all types of goods—grain, cloth, wool, weapons, armor, spices, glass, wine—throughout Europe and the Mediterranean, and from loaning and investing money.

The massive eight-sided dome of the city cathedral in Florence, Italy, was built during the Renaissance, and it still dominates the city center. Wealth brought in by trade and banking paid for spectacular buildings, which architects modeled on ancient Roman forms.

They invented new ways to keep track of how their business was doing. They hired weavers to make fine woolen cloth that could be sold at high prices in the markets and bazaars of Europe, western Asia, and North Africa. They hired shipbuilders to design and construct ships that were bigger, faster, and more seaworthy than earlier models, which meant more merchandise and fewer shipwrecks. Through these business activities, merchants created the economic system based on private ownership, competition, and profit that later spread to most of the world and came to be called capitalism. The Black Death hit Italian cities very hard—Florence lost at least half its population—but it did not destroy their prosperity.

Ambitious merchants gained political power to match their economic power. They bought, fought, or negotiated freedom for their cities from the nobles who had earlier controlled these areas. These free cities were ruled by city councils, and wealthy merchant families dominated these councils. At the time that Leonardo came to Florence, the city council and the city were under the control of Lorenzo de' Medici, whose family had made an enormous fortune in banking. Lorenzo was "a great and extraordinary genius" who showed "boundless generosity" to "talented men," according to a city history of Florence written in 1509, and deserved the title people gave him: Lorenzo the Magnificent.

Lorenzo was not the only wealthy man who spent money on talent. Financial success meant that Italian merchants had money for such luxuries as art and music, and made them interested in anything that would lead to still greater success. One of those things was education. Most education in the 12th and 13th centuries in Europe was organized by the Catholic Church, and was designed to train monks, priests, and nuns so they could copy religious manuscripts, recite prayers, serve as church officials, or study the Bible. Universities trained doctors and lawyers along with philosophers and church officials, but their numbers were very small and they learned more about theories than about practical issues. Doctors learned about the influence of blood on disease, but not how to treat a patient, and lawyers learned about laws, but not how to argue a case in court.

Wealthy merchant and arts patron Lorenzo de' Medici (center) is surrounded by a group of artists whose work he paid for, including, on the right, the young Michelangelo. The painter put the group in a classical setting with pillars and an elaborate ceiling to show off his skills at recreating the ancient past. The elaborate ceiling and the landscape in the background show off his skills in creating perspective.

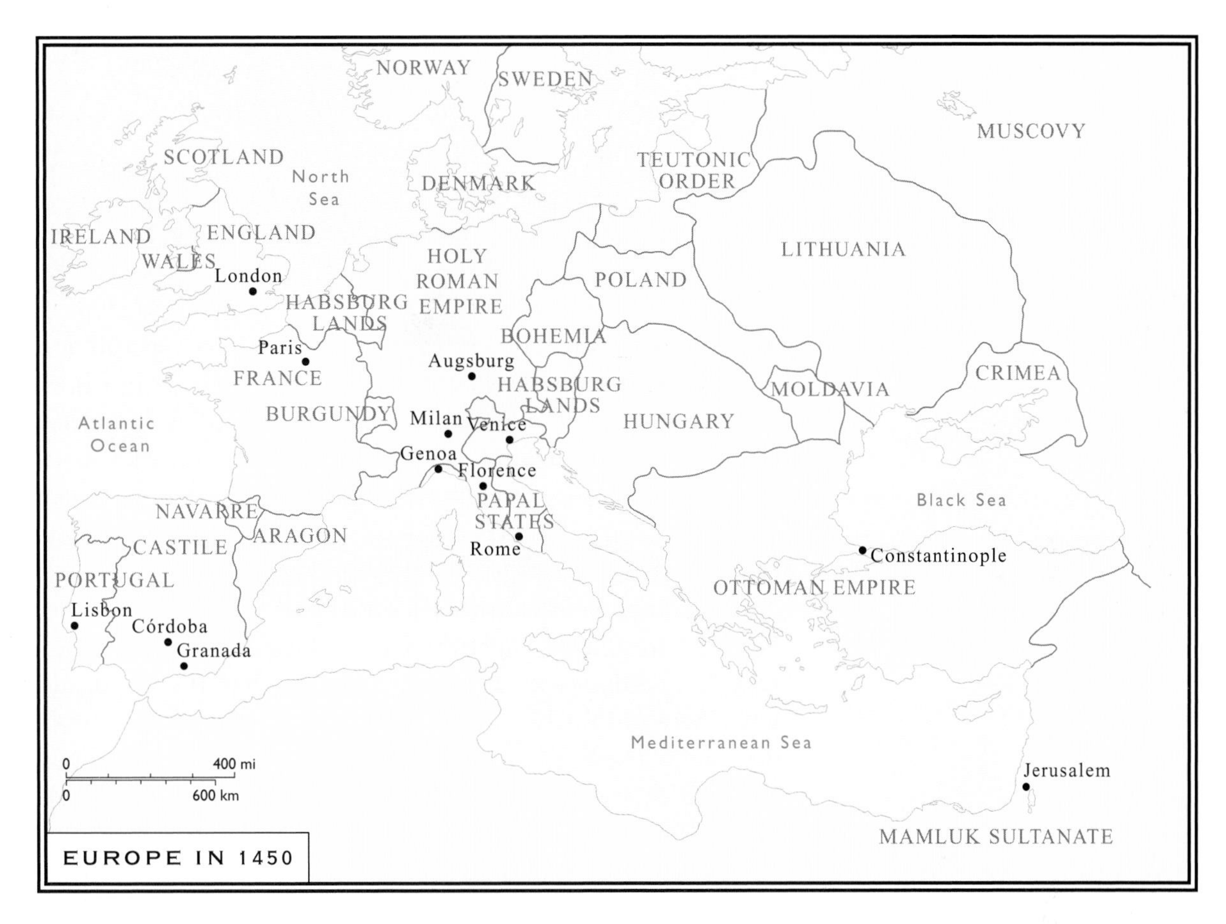

EUROPE IN 1450

In Florence and other booming cities such as Venice, scholars and teachers proposed a new type of education that they called "new learning" or humanism. We might expect "new learning" to involve laboratory discoveries or practical education, but this new learning focused on the writings of ancient Latin and Greek authors. These classics provided models of how to write clearly, argue effectively, and speak persuasively, important skills for future diplomats, lawyers, military leaders, businessmen, or politicians. Studying the "humanities," as this course of study was called, provided practical skills and also moral lessons for society's future leaders.

Merchants and bankers sent their sons to humanist schools, and ambitious young men from outside Italy flocked to these schools or to ones that were opened later in their

The prince ought to read histories, and to consider in them the actions of excellent men.

—Niccolò Machiavelli, *The Prince*, 1513

own cities. Humanist teachers and their ideas spread out from Florence across the Alps, and eventually to northern European cities such as London and Paris. A few humanist fathers even taught their daughters Latin and Greek.

One of the creators of humanism, the 14th-century Italian scholar and poet Francesco Petrarch, was especially interested in the classical Greek and Roman past. As one of his admirers described him in a biography written in 1436, Petrarch "restored to light the ancient elegance of style which was lost and dead." Petrarch thought that the thousand years between the decline of the Roman Empire and his own day were "Dark Ages" of gloom and barbarity. He searched through dusty monastery libraries and private collections for the works of ancient Roman writers, and shared the writings he found with other scholars. He and other writers studied these Latin classics to learn about human nature.

A Game of Chess, *painted in 1555 by Sofonisba Anguissola, shows the artist's three younger sisters and their servant. It was difficult for women during the Renaissance to get artistic training, and the few who did, including Anguissola, were usually daughters of painters and learned from their fathers.*

Italian artists, who had the ruins of the ancient Roman Empire all around them, began to use Roman buildings as inspiration for their own designs. They carved statues that showed realistic human forms like those of the ancient Greeks and Romans. In bringing the glories of ancient Greece and Rome back to life, these scholars and artists thought they were overcoming the "dark" or "middle" ages, and creating a new golden age. This new age came to be called the Renaissance, which means "rebirth." In studying the classical past and the people of their own day, humanists were especially interested in individuals who had risen above their background to become brilliant, powerful, or unique. They wrote biographies of ambitious rulers such as Lorenzo de' Medici, honored scholars such as Petrarch, and talented artists such as Leonardo.

YOU'RE A GENIUS!

The humanists' emphasis on individual talent influenced artists, who came to believe that their skill at painting or sculpting was the result not simply of good training, but also of their personal genius. Renaissance artists were the first to paint self-portraits and to sign their works of art. The name and abilities of a brilliant artist such as Leonardo became recognized all over Europe, and many people wanted to hire him because of who he was, not just what he could do.

Leonardo was not only a painter, but also an engineer. He was hired by rulers in Italy and France, and even the pope, to design practical things, including weapons, fortresses, and water systems, as well as to make works of art. He was also a scientist. Trying to understand how the human body worked, Leonardo studied live and dead bodies, doing autopsies and dissections to investigate muscles and the circulation of the blood. He carefully analyzed the effects of light, using what he learned to paint strong contrasts of light and shadow, and he experimented with perspective, or how you show three dimensions on a flat, or two-dimensional, surface. He tested new materials for painting and sculpture, some of which worked, and some of which did not. His painting of the Last Supper shows powerful human expressions in a way that influenced many later artists, but the paint began to flake off the wall as soon as it was finished, and the painting has had to be restored many times.

This self-portrait was painted by the German artist Albrecht Dürer when he was 13 years old. Dürer was the first painter to describe the concept of artistic genius, and he painted a series of self-portraits that give insight into his personality.

Leonardo was someone whose genius was recognized by many artists and rulers, but the highest public praise went to another artist from Florence, Michelangelo Buonarotti. Michelangelo (also always known by his first name) was born and raised in Florence. He became an apprentice to a painter when he was 12, and several years later began working as a sculptor. His earliest surviving sculpture is a battle scene that he carved when he was about 16 years old. Lorenzo de' Medici recognized his talent and invited the teenaged artist to stay at his palace. When he was about 20, Michelangelo went to Rome, where the pope and other wealthy church leaders wanted art that showed the power of the church and the power of their own families. Michelangelo's largest and greatest painting was on the ceiling and altar wall of the Sistine Chapel in the palace of the pope,

Drawings of machinery from Leonardo's notebooks. Leonardo drew designs for many types of inventions, some of which were built right away. Others, including a helicopter, parachute, tank, and machine gun, were not manufactured until centuries later.

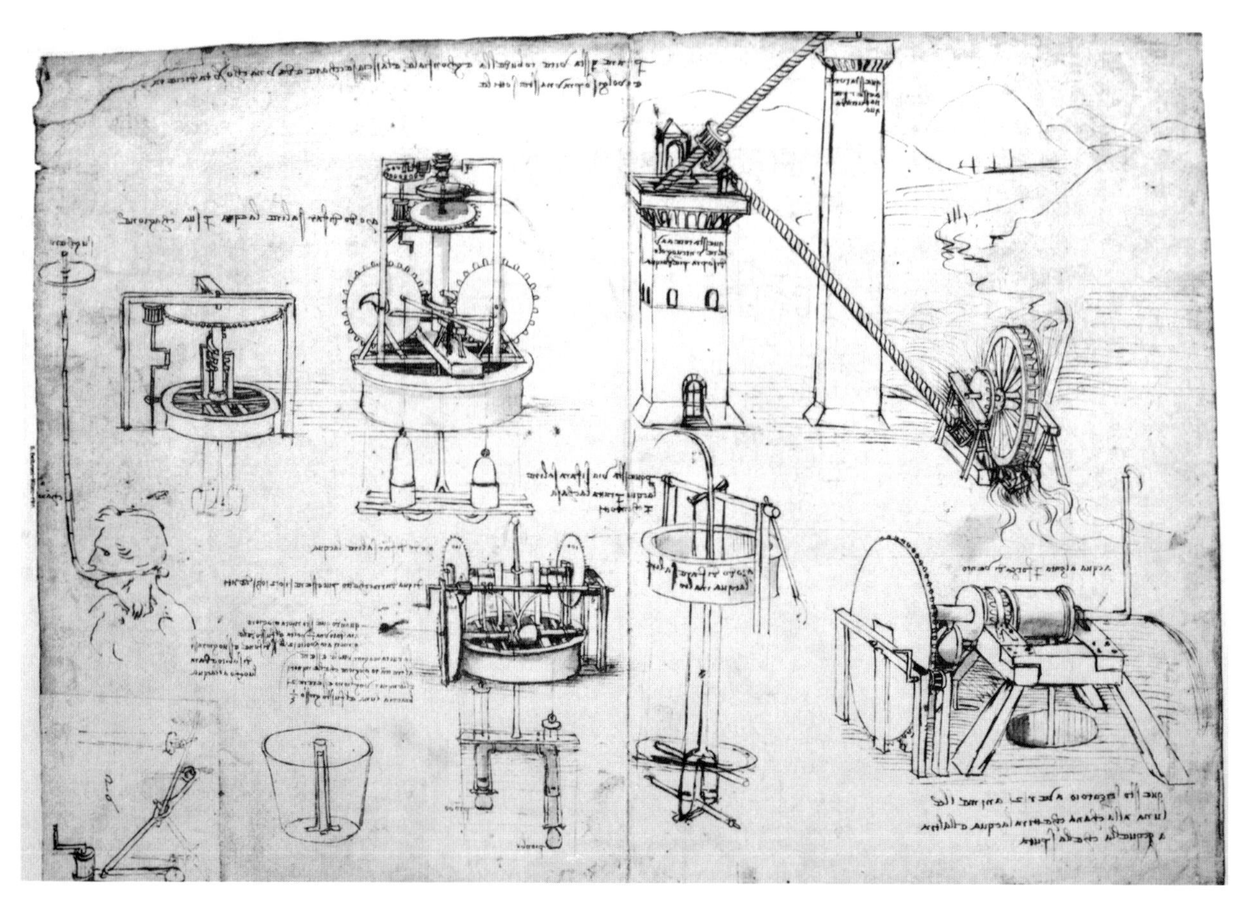

The Wondrous Works of Nature

LEONARDO DA VINCI, NOTEBOOKS, 1480s–1510s

Leonardo da Vinci planned to write books on many subjects, including anatomy, painting, human movement, and the flight of birds, but he never finished any of them. His writings survive mostly in the form of notebooks, many of them written in backward "mirror writing," which Leonardo taught himself to keep other people from reading his words easily. These notebooks also contain drawings of people, animals, and inventions, with the writing wedged in between. The notebooks themselves are scattered in many public museums and libraries in Europe, though sections of them have been published in the last hundred years or so.

The mind of the painter must resemble a mirror, which always takes the color of the object it reflects. . . . Therefore you must know, O painter! That you cannot be a good one if you are not the universal master of representing by your art every kind of form produced by nature. . . . The eye, which is called the window of the soul, is the principle means by which the central sense can most completely and abundantly appreciate the infinite works of nature; and the ear is the second, which acquires dignity by hearing of the things the eye has seen. If you, historians or poets or mathematicians, had not seen things with your eyes you could not report of them in writing. . . . We, by our arts, may be called the grandsons of God.

And you, O Man, who will discern in this work of mine the wondrous works of nature, if you think it would be a criminal thing to destroy it, reflect how much more criminal it is to take the life of a man, and if this, his external form, appears to you marvelously constructed, remember that it is nothing as compared with the soul that dwells in that structure; for that indeed is a thing divine.

Leonardo sketched his idea for a parachute in a notebook.

Michelangelo painted the Last Judgment *over a five-year period from 1536 to 1541. The dramatic scene of Christ fiercely commanding tombs to open shows a very different side of Renaissance art than Leonardo's calm* Mona Lisa.

which shows great power and intense feeling in the human body. It is difficult to look at his paintings or statues without being moved by the tension, sorrow, or anger they contain. He was sometimes criticized for showing too much raw emotion and drama, especially in *The Last Judgment,* a gigantic painting on the wall of the Sistine Chapel that shows souls rising to heaven or being dragged to hell.

Both Michelangelo and Leonardo trained in the way that most artists did, by being apprenticed to older artists and assisting in their workshops. Great art might be a matter of "genius," but artists were still expected to be well trained, and they spent years copying drawings and paintings, learning how to prepare paint, and reading books about design and composition. Once they were adults, Michelangelo and many other artists were known for their large and well-run workshops, where younger artists sometimes assisted the master with the easier parts of large paintings, such as backgrounds and clothing and other fabrics.

Artistic works, whether single portraits or huge buildings, were usually created for specific people called patrons—merchants, city councils, rulers, or churches—who ordered and paid for them. The military leaders who ruled many Italian cities during the Renaissance ordered elaborate armor etched with battle scenes, had portraits painted or statues erected of themselves in that armor, and had huge palaces constructed where they could entertain lavishly. Wealthy nobles and merchants had artists paint religious scenes that included themselves and their families as onlookers, or even participants. One Renaissance nativity scene shows three members of the Medici family, the rulers of Florence, as the three wise men presenting gifts to the infant Jesus.

Patrons sometimes wanted to make sure they were getting what they paid for, and so got very involved in the artist's work. Pope Julius II, for example, demanded that Michelangelo work as fast as he could on painting the ceiling of the Sistine Chapel in Rome. Michelangelo painted on wet plaster—a technique called fresco—from a scaffolding, standing up, and he wrote a poem complaining of a stiff neck and of paint dripping into his eyes: "My painting all the day doth drop a rich mosaic on my face." Artists like Michelangelo may have created the art for which the Renaissance is known, but wealthy and powerful people like Julius paid for it.

THE PRINCE, A SPANISH GENTLEMAN, AND THE GREATEST PLAYWRIGHT WHO EVER LIVED

Before the 15th century, most art in Europe was religious, and many writers focused on piety, prayer, and achieving salvation. By contrast, Renaissance humanists and artists agreed that the people and objects of *this* world were important, and that a person didn't have to give up the material world in order to live a good life. No one in the Renaissance denied the existence of God or the importance of religion, however. Talents should be developed, genius honored, wealth enjoyed, and beauty celebrated, they thought, because all these things came from God. Italian merchants shared this point of view, and many began their business records with the phrase "in the name of God and of profit."

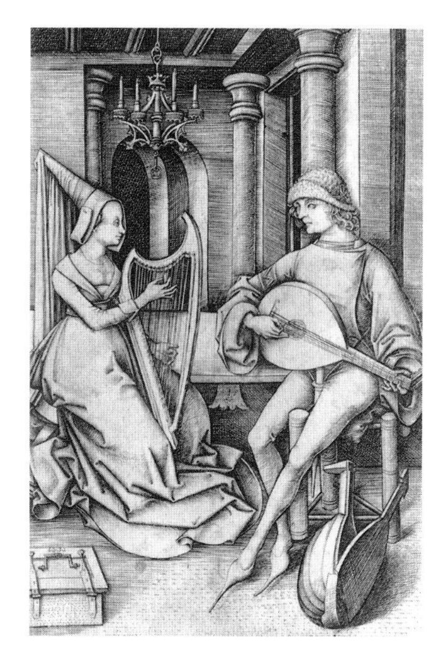

A courtier and court lady play a duet on harp and lute. During the Renaissance, composers began to write new types of music for secular occasions such as dances, plays, and wedding banquets, though they also continued to compose religious music.

Were there limits on what a great individual could or should do? This was a question that troubled Niccolò Machiavelli, especially when it came to individuals who had power over others. Machiavelli was born in Florence, where he became a government official and writer. When a new group of leaders gained power, his political career was ruined and he was banished from the city. This gave him lots of time to write and think, and what he thought most

Machiavelli used this desk when he was in exile from Florence and writing The Prince. *Political feuds in Italy often led to one of the feuding groups being exiled, and exile was also a common punishment for people found guilty of crimes.*

about was politics. In his best-known book, *The Prince,* Machiavelli argues that the function of a ruler (or any government) is to preserve order and security. To do this the ruler should use whatever means he needs, including brutality, lying, and manipulation, because a ruler's moral code is not the same as a private person's. Effective rulers have what Machiavelli calls *virtù*, which is not "virtue" like it sounds, but rather the ability to shape the world around them according to their will.

This emphasis on a ruler's force and deceit led people later to use the word "Machiavellian" to mean cunning and ruthless, but Machiavelli himself did not say that rulers can do anything they want. "It is much safer for the prince to be feared than loved," Machiavelli advised, "but he ought to avoid making himself hated." In addition, even the best-prepared and most merciless ruler with lots of *virtù* was still under the power of Fate, who could turn against him at any point for no apparent reason.

Though Machiavelli's ideas—or ideas people said came from Machiavelli—were often seen as immoral, they described actual politics in the Italy of Machiavelli's day very well. In his banishment from Florence, Machiavelli himself experienced how cruel fate could be, and throughout Italy military leaders attacked and conquered cities, defeating the weaker armies of city councils. The new rulers hired humanist scholars, along with poets, artists, and musicians, to glorify themselves and their families. These Italian courts served as models for the kings and queens of Spain, France, and England, who hired Italian or home-grown humanists as teachers, diplomats, lawyers, and writers, and supported artists, musicians, and architects.

Such well-educated people throughout Europe communicated with one another in Latin, the language in which scholars and authors wrote their serious works. Some authors—including many trained in the classics—also began to write in the languages spoken every day by people in Europe. They wrote poetry, plays, and stories in Italian, French, Spanish, German, and English that were often much more popular than their works in Latin. These languages became literary languages as well as spoken ones.

Italian was the first modern European language to become a literary language, with the writings of Petrarch, Boccaccio, and the earlier Florentine writer Dante Alighieri. A group of poets who wrote in Italian gathered at the court of Lorenzo de' Medici in Florence in the 1480s, including the young artist Michelangelo. These poets all celebrated love and beauty, for why else, as Michelangelo wrote in "Love's Justification," "has God made the world which we inhabit?"

In France and Spain, many authors wrote poetry and romantic stories of knights and ladies in the everyday language of their countries. The Spanish author Miguel de Cervantes began his career writing romances and plays, but toward the end of his life wrote *Don Quixote,* often regarded as the greatest masterpiece in all Spanish literature. *Don Quixote* tells the story of the idealistic country gentleman Don Quixote and his faithful squire Sancho Panza, who encounter every kind of person in Spanish society as Don Quixote tries to right wrongs and rescue his beloved lady from (largely imaginary) dangers. The story is both funny and sad, and asks very basic questions—is it good to have grand dreams, or are these "castles in the air" that "lead us

You live happily and
know no sorrow
thinking only of your
newly acquired fame.
We remain, with fear in
our heart and
grief on our brow for you;
sister longs for
brother, wife for husband,
mother for son.

—Italian humanist poet Vittoria Colonna, "Epistle to her Husband after the Battle of Ravenna," 1512, when her husband was still away at war.

> *Fair is youth and void*
> *of sorrow*
> *But it hourly flies away*
> *Youths and maids enjoy*
> *today*
> *Nought ye know about*
> *tomorrow.*
>
> —Lorenzo de' Medici,
> "A Carnival Song", 1470s
> or 1480s

on a wild goose chase"? Can we ever have "too much of a good thing?" Should "every man look before he leaps" or does "faint heart never win fair lady?" All these familiar expressions come from *Don Quixote,* which has been translated into most of the world's languages and turned into plays, operas, ballets, and a popular musical, *The Man of La Mancha.* Cervantes himself had the kind of life and adventures that Don Quixote only dreamt of—he fought and was wounded in a major naval battle, was captured by pirates,

D. Francisci Petrarcae poetae laureati
Triumphi sex incipit et primo primu
quod de amore inscribitur:

NEL TEMPO
CHE RINOVA
I MIEI SOSPIRI

Per la dolce memoria di quel giorno

A handwritten copy of Francesco Petrarch's The Triumph of Love. *The copyist wrote the introduction at the top in scholarly Latin, but the poem itself, which begins with the decorated letter N, is in Italian, which more people could read.*

sold as a slave, and eventually ransomed at a price that would ruin his family. He hoped to raise money by writing, but he wasn't very successful at this.

Don Quixote reached a wide audience, but plays reached even more people. All sorts of plays were put on as part of church holidays or city festivals, by local groups or traveling companies of actors. Towns sometimes competed to write and put on the best play. There were plays showing Bible stories or the lives of the saints, and plays about heroic dragon-slayers, doomed lovers, and miserly merchants. Wandering performers used puppets, trained animals, and acrobatic tricks to attract viewers, and sometimes pulled teeth and sold medicine in addition to providing entertainment. In traveling troupes, actors and actresses dressed up as certain stock characters, with improvised dialogue, sweeping gestures, and lots of physical comedy. The word slapstick, in fact, comes from the stick carried by one of these characters, Harlequin, a mischievous servant dressed in diamond-patterned tights who is often shown as the joker in modern decks of cards.

A poster advertises a 19th-century French opera based on Don Quixote. *Cervantes wrote* Don Quixote *as a novel, but its sympathetic characters, eccentric hero, and humorous plot twists make it a perfect story to be told through opera, musicals, or ballet.*

Plays of all types were very popular in England, especially in London, where public theaters offered entertainment for rich and poor. Beginning in the late 15th century, the theaters of London staged the plays of William Shakespeare, who is often described as the greatest playwright who ever lived. Shakespeare came from a middle-class background in a medium-sized town and probably attended elementary school and learned some Latin, but had no more formal education. He married and had three children, then went to London, where he became an actor and playwright for the Lord Chamberlain's Men, a company of professional actors. He later became the part-owner of several London theaters and spent most of the rest of his life in London, writing plays and playing minor roles in them.

A traveler sketched a drawing of the Swan Theatre in London in 1595. Elizabethan theaters were roofless; wealthy people sat along the sides in covered boxes, which protected them somewhat from the weather, while common people stood in front of the stage for the whole performance.

Shakespeare's talent was so great that some people have doubted whether someone with so little formal training could actually have written the plays. However, most people think that he did write them, and that Shakespeare's use of humanist style and classical plots—stories about the ancient Roman emperor Julius Caesar or the Egyptian queen Cleopatra—show how widely humanist education had spread. By Shakespeare's time, not only did wealthy merchants' sons in Florence or London have the chance to learn the classics and the power of great language, but quite ordinary boys in very ordinary towns did as well. Shakespeare also learned on his own about the huge variety of subjects that appear in his plays, including music, the law, the Bible, hunting, military tactics, art, politics, the sea, history, and sports. Shakespeare's plays have people from all walks of life—wise fools, foolish kings, greedy daughters, cunning thieves, cowardly soldiers, proud generals, boastful drunkards, and stupid officials. In *Hamlet, The Prince of Denmark,* Shakespeare gives Hamlet lines that seem to summarize Renaissance ideas about humans and their talents: "What a piece of work is a man! How noble in reason! How infinite in faculty! In form, in moving, how express and admirable! In action how like an angel! In apprehension how like a god!" However, these lines are spoken in a scene where people are trying to figure out whether Hamlet is insane or just pretending to be, so we cannot be sure that Shakespeare meant the lines to be taken literally. Like Mona Lisa's smile, they make us want to know more about Hamlet and about the author who invented him.

CHAPTER 3

GHOSTS, MONKEYS, OR CONFUCIUS

LEARNING AS POWER IN MING CHINA

A young woman from a prominent family falls in love with a young man of whom her parents disapprove. She dies of grief, and the young man is heartbroken. William Shakespeare told this familiar story in *Romeo and Juliet*. At the end of that play Romeo poisons himself when he thinks Juliet is dead, and then Juliet stabs herself with Romeo's dagger when she sees his dead body. "Never was a story of more woe, than this of Juliet and her Romeo," say the play's final lines. At almost exactly the same time, halfway around the world, the Chinese playwright Tang Xianzu told a similar story of love and family conflict in *The Peony Pavilion*.

Actresses in a modern production of The Peony Pavilion *wear costumes similar to those that were worn in Ming China. Du Liniang (left) walks with her maid in the garden, where she sees the beauty of nature and dreams of her beloved.*

This play tells the story of Du Liniang, the daughter of a high-ranking official who keeps her shut away in the house. While on a walk in the family garden, she dreams of a young scholar named Liu Mengmei and falls in love with him. When she wakes up, she knows that the dream will never come true, and dies of a broken heart. Three years later, the real Liu Mengmei finds Du Liniang's portrait, meets her ghost, and falls in love with her. Instead of killing himself like Romeo does when he thinks Juliet is dead, Liu Mengmei knows the woman he loves is dead, but, following the instructions of her ghost, opens her grave anyway. Out comes Du Liniang as a beautiful living woman, with

Ah, the way of the many sages,
Is all collected right here,
If you cannot reflect deeply and study hard,
Then these books will be empty tools.

—Scholar-official Fang Xiaoru, poem to his bookshelf, 1397

the chorus singing "only the happy bride knows all there is to know." They defy the tradition of obeying one's father, get married, and, as we would say, "live happily ever after."

William Shakespeare and Tang Xianzu did not know one another, of course, but there are more similarities in their lives and their writing than just one play about star-crossed lovers. Both of them were from middle-class backgrounds. Both of them loved language and used it exuberantly and playfully. Both of them often based their plays on stories they had read but developed the personalities of their characters more fully and made the plots more complicated than in the original stories. Both of them wrote plays that are still performed today and made into movies. The times and places where the writers lived also had similarities. In Shakespeare's Renaissance England, business was growing, education focused on the classical past, and artists were creating new styles of art. The same was true in Tang Xianzu's Ming China.

THE EMPEROR'S NEW IDEA

The founding of the Ming dynasty would have made a good plot for one of Shakespeare's history plays. Zhu Yuanzhang was from a poor peasant family. After his parents and brothers died of the plague, he lived in a Buddhist monastery and begged on the streets to survive. This peasant boy grew up to lead one of the many rebel armies fighting against the Mongol rulers of China. Zhu became an effective and brutal military leader, and his forces slowly defeated those of the other warlords. His armies conquered most of China, defeating both the Chinese and Mongol armies. In 1368 they conquered the Mongol capital of Khanbalik in northern China, and Zhu declared himself emperor, taking the name Hongwu for his reign. He called his new dynasty, or hereditary line of rulers, "Ming," meaning brilliant.

The Hongwu emperor immediately attempted to rid China of everything that reminded people of their conquest by the Mongols. Mongol palaces were looted, Mongol names were taken out of court records, and traditional

Chinese robes and long braids replaced Mongol jackets and shorter haircuts. The new emperor was not well educated, but he decided that education in the ideas of the ancient Chinese philosopher Confucius was the core of Chinese culture. High positions in government, he said, should go to scholars who could best prove their knowledge of Confucian ideas.

Why were the ideas of Confucius so attractive? Confucius was born in the middle of the 6th century BCE, a turbulent period in Chinese history. His parents died while he was a child, and he developed ideas about how to end the violence he saw around him. Confucius decided that the best way to keep a society peaceful and prosperous was to make sure that only wise and honest men held positions of power. These men should be sincere and ethical, respect their fathers and their rulers, honor their ancestors and the past, and be devoted to public service. The superiority of these wise and honest men came to them naturally, but it was further enhanced through education.

Confucius said that rulers should have these qualities, and they should surround themselves with advisors who were also wise and moral. Under the leadership of such advisors, society would be a well-ordered hierarchy in which everyone was arranged in ranks and knew their place. The educated would rule the common people, parents would rule their children, and men would rule women. Women were considered important because of their role as homemakers and mothers, especially as the mothers of sons who would carry on the family line. But they were always bound by

The ancient philosopher Confucius sits in a fancy chair, dressed as a scholar. For thousands of years, people in China revered Confucius for his wisdom and often had paintings or small statues of him in their homes.

what Confucius called the "Three Obediences"—to their fathers, their husbands, and their sons. These hierarchies were not to be upset, argued Confucius in his writings, known as the *Analects* ("sayings"), because "the relation between superiors and inferiors is like that between wind and grass. The grass must bend when the wind blows across it."

Confucius's ideas were almost unknown when he died, but his writings were not lost. In the same way that scholars in Italy such as Petrarch rediscovered their own classical past, later Chinese thinkers found and built on Confucius's ideas. Many emperors approved of their emphasis on hierarchy, respect for authority, and public service, and they established a system of civil service examinations, which tested young men's knowledge in Confucian philosophy, law, and literature.

These exams could be grueling, and guards watched candidates closely to prevent cheating. Academies were set up to train young men for these examinations, and those who scored well were given high offices, government salaries, and special titles. Many of these scholar-officials came from wealthy noble families who could afford the best schools, but some of them were bright commoners who rose in prominence on the basis of their ability. Tang Xianzu's fictional hero Liu Mengmei is just such a poor but smart young man and is, in fact, on his way to take the exam when he sees the ghost of Du Liniang.

Success in the exams could lead to a steady job and a good income, but officials who strayed from the Confucian

If we do not teach them [people] concretely and sincerely to devote themselves to the task of doing good and removing evil... all that they do will not be genuine.

—Confucian scholar-official Wang Yangming,
Instruction for a Practical Living, 1520

Confucian scholars gather in a garden in springtime for a learned discussion, assisted by their students. The student on the left is preparing brushes, paints, and ink, and the students on the right are carrying games.

principles of hierarchy and respect for authority could get into trouble. Officials found to be dishonest were beaten publicly in front of the emperor and his court. These beatings could be severe enough to kill them, and others died from the humiliation and dishonor of this public shaming. Loyalty to one emperor might also not be welcomed by the next. Fang Xiaoru was the highest scholarly authority in all China at the beginning of the 15th century and an advisor to the emperor. That emperor disappeared in a bloody civil war, and the new emperor demanded that Fang Xiaoru declare his support for him. When Fang refused, the emperor executed him and killed all his family members and associates as well, more than several hundred people. Even having some of Fang's writings meant execution.

Thinkers such as the scholar-official Wang Yangming in the 16th century expanded Confucian principles, seeking to apply them to every aspect of life. Like Renaissance humanists in Europe, these later Confucian thinkers (called neo-Confucians, which means "new Confucians") sought to revive a way of thinking they thought was ideal, and

continues on page 48

Young People Should Know Their Place

CONFUCIAN ELDER, INSTRUCTION MANUAL FOR HOW TO RUN A HOUSEHOLD, LATE 16TH CENTURY

In the late 16th century, one of the elders in the wealthy Miu family gave the following directions to his kinsmen on how to run their households. The author, whose name we do not know, thought that the Confucian principles of hierarchy, respect for one's elders, duty, and moderation should be followed in family life.

Observe the rituals and proprieties

2. Marriage arrangements should not be made final by the presenting of betrothal gifts until the boy and girl have both reached thirteen; otherwise, time might bring changes which cause regrets.

6. Not celebrating one's birthday has since ancient times been regarded as an exemplary virtue. An exception is the birthdays of those who are beyond their sixty-first year, which should be celebrated by their sons and grandsons.

7. On reaching five, a boy should be taught to recite the primers and not be allowed to show arrogance or laziness. On reaching six, a girl should be taught *Admonitions for Women* [a book of advice for girls and women] and not be allowed to venture out of her chamber. If children are frequently given snacks and playfully entertained, their nature will be spoiled and they will grow up to be unruly and bad. This can be prevented if caught at an early age.

Exercise restraint

1. Our young people should know their place and observe correct manners. They are not permitted to gamble, to fight, to engage in lawsuits, or to deal in salt privately. Such unlawful acts will only lead to their own downfall.

3. Pride is a dangerous trait. Those who pride themselves on wealth, rank, or learning are inviting evil consequences. Even if one's accomplishments are indeed unique, there is no need to press them on anyone else.

5. Just as diseases are caused by what goes into one's mouth, misfortunes are caused by what comes out of one's mouth. Those who are immoderate in eating and unrestrained in speaking have no one else to blame for their own ruin.

6. Most men lack resolve and listen to what their women say. As a result, blood relatives become estranged and competitiveness, suspicion and distance arise between them. Therefore, when a wife first comes

into a family, it should be made clear to her that such things are prohibited. "Start teaching one's son when he is a baby, start teaching one's daughter-in-law when she first arrives." That is to say, preventive measures should be taken early.

7. "A family's fortune can be foretold from whether its members are early risers" is a maxim of the ancient sages. Everyone, male and female, should rise before dawn and should not go to bed until after the first drum. Never should they indulge themselves in a false sense of security and leisure, for such behavior will eventually lead them to poverty.

8. Young family members who deliberately violate family regulations should be taken to the family temple, have their offenses reported to the ancestors, and be severely punished. They should then be taught to improve themselves. Those who do not accept punishment or persist in their wrongdoings will bring harm to themselves.

An artist painted a respectful portrait of his great-grand-uncle at age 85, an age that very few people would have reached in Ming China. Confucian teachings urged family members to honor their ancestors and value the elderly.

Preserve the Family Property

3. Books constitute the lifeline of a family. A record should be kept of their titles. They should be aired out at regular intervals, stored in a high chamber, and kept from being dispersed. In this way we can keep intact our ancestors' writings.

6. In order to cultivate the moral character of the young, one must severely punish those who are so unruly that they have no sense of righteousness or who so indulge their desires that they destroy their own health. One should also correct those who have improper hobbies, such as making too many friends and avoiding work, indulging in playing musical instruments and the game of Go, collecting art and valuables, composing music, singing, or dancing. All these hobbies destroy a person's ambition. Those who indulge in them may consider themselves free spirits; yet little do they know that these hobbies are their most harmful enemies.

8. Scholars, farmers, artisans, and merchants all hold respectable occupations. Scholarship ranks the highest; farming is next; and then craft and business. However, it should be up to the individual to measure his ability against his aspirations as well as to find the most suitable occupation for himself.

The Great Wall of China winds across the mountains north of Beijing. The sections built by the Ming emperors snake through thousands of miles of remote and rugged territory, and were manned by imperial guards.

continued from page 45

looked to the past for guidance in how to turn knowledge into action. They saw the best life as one of service, and regarded the natural world as something to be studied and understood, much like Leonardo did. As Wang Yangming wrote in *The Great Learning* in 1525, "Heaven, Earth, the myriad things, and man form one body," unified by "the clear intelligence of the human mind." For much of his life, Wang had plenty of time to develop his own "clear intelligence" because he was banished from the emperor's court for insulting a powerful official.

Wise and moral leaders were expected to concern themselves with practical problems, and the best of the Ming emperors did this. To keep out the Mongols, they extended and reinforced the Great Wall. Walls had been built to keep out northern invaders since about 200 BCE, but by the beginning of the Ming dynasty most of them were in ruins. The Ming emperors built much longer and sturdier walls, extending the main wall to more than two thousand miles, a job that took hundreds of thousands of workers. Most of the Great Wall that you can see and walk on today was built during the Ming dynasty. It worked quite well at keeping out bandits and small military forces, but was not very helpful in resisting large invasions.

> *He was of a pure and good-hearted natural disposition... He managed domestic affairs in a diligent and frugal fashion. He had his ways of making money, from which his family could increase its wealth... he repeatedly organized famine relief measures.*
>
> —Inscription on the tomb of Ming-era merchant Wang Zhen, 1495

MING'S BEAUTIFUL THINGS

The first two centuries of the Ming dynasty were times of economic expansion and population growth. Chinese merchant ships traveled all over the South China Sea, and in the early 15th century, the third Ming emperor, who took the reign name Yongle, sent the Chinese navy as far as the Indian Ocean and Persian Gulf to demonstrate Chinese power. The Yongle emperor came to power through the violent overthrow of his nephew, the rightful heir, but he also supported scholarship, commissioning 2,000 scholars to write a vast encyclopedia on all subjects, This work took five years and more than 11,000 manuscript volumes. Trade, also encouraged by the emperor, brought wealth, and one official reported in his "Essay on Merchants" in the 1570s that "the profits from the tea and salt trades are especially great."

This piece of Chinese paper money from about 1375 CE was worth 1,000 brass coins. A growing population and expanding economy increased the need for new types of money, so the government printed paper money as well as minting coins. It was quite easy to counterfeit paper money, and this bill includes a warning against counterfeiting.

Farmers planted new types of rice that grew quickly, along with mulberry trees, which provided the food for silk worms. In the middle of the 16th century, Spanish and Portuguese merchants brought peanuts, sweet potatoes, and corn from the Americas. These crops could be grown on poor soil without irrigation, and they provided important vitamins and protein to the steadily growing Chinese population. By 1600, there were more than 120 million people in China, and many large cities.

Just as they did in Renaissance Europe, wealthy merchants, landowners, and political leaders wanted to surround themselves with beautiful things. This included fine porcelain fired in a kiln at extremely high temperatures, a process invented in China during the artistic flowering in the Tang dynasty of 618–907. Porcelain is both strong and delicate, and it gained the name "china" from the land of its origin. During the Ming dynasty, porcelain makers perfected blue and white patterns for dishes and vases that were wildly popular first in China and then in other parts of the world. They were so popular that European porcelain makers later copied them, making their own blue and white dishes.

Wealthy households also bought lacquerware—boxes, dishes, trays, and other items usually made of wood and coated with many layers of varnish so that they are waterproof and durable. The technique of making lacquerware, which could involve as many as two hundred coats of varnish, first developed in China, and then spread to Japan. In the 16th century, lacquerware dishes, screens, boxes, and chests began to be traded around the world, and these beautiful objects became status symbols.

Painters during the Ming period used techniques and styles that had been created in earlier eras. In addition to pictures, their paintings often included brief poems or sayings written in calligraphy, or fine handwriting. Painting and calligraphy were done with the same flexible brush and sometimes the same ink, so artists wrote poems as part of their paintings. Dramatic landscapes were a favorite subject, which fit with neo-Confucian ideas about the value of studying nature. These landscapes often included very small figures, such as travelers on a road dwarfed by rugged mountains or a scholar under a tree next to a rushing river contemplating the scene around him. Humans are clearly part of nature in these paintings, but not the center of attention. Artists saw the object they painted, whether it was a landscape, a grove of bamboo, a flower, a bird, or an animal, as a means of revealing their personality. The poems they wrote to accompany the scene demonstrated their learning and made their paintings even more personal. Some artists painted scenes that included visual depictions of nicknames people had given them, so that the paintings included an inside joke that only their friends would understand.

Many artists in the Ming era were Confucian scholars who painted as a way of expressing themselves, not professionals who

A fierce dragon with outstretched claws, symbolizing immortality and power, crawls around a blue-and-white porcelain vase from the Ming dynasty. Porcelain vases, cups, and dishes could be found in every wealthy home in China, and were later exported around the world.

supported themselves by painting. We might call them "Renaissance men," as they were expected to do many things well. Wen Zhenming was one of these, born into a wealthy aristocratic family who gave him a good education in literature, philosophy, and calligraphy. He painted landscapes, animals, and human figures, usually including a poem that heightened the mood. Tang Yin was not as lucky as his friend Wen. He was a bright young man from a middle-class family, and, like any young man wanting to get ahead in Ming China, he took the imperial civil service examinations. He was accused of cheating and spent some time in prison waiting for trial. (In both Europe and China at this time, prisons held more people awaiting trial than people who had been convicted.) His lack of family money meant he had to support himself by selling his paintings, which made wealthier scholar-artists look down on him.

Not all Confucian scholars could paint, but all of them were expected to write in an elegant style and produce philosophy, poetry, or history that would teach moral lessons. More people could read in the Ming era than earlier in Chinese history, but they did not want to spend all their time reading serious works. Instead they read short stories written in simple language that told about people like themselves who fell in love, helped their neighbors, fought with their families, or opposed corrupt officials. Or they read novels such as *The Golden Lotus,* the story of a tyrant who bribes officials, gambles, and marries many wives. People especially liked *The Journey to the West,* often called *The Monkey King,* written by the scholar-official Wu Ch'eng-en.

The Monkey King is based on the story of a real 7th-century Chinese monk named Xuanzang who traveled to India in search of Buddhist holy books. Wu wove legends and monster stories into his version of Xuanzang's journey. Wu's hero frees the Monkey King, a mythical creature skilled in

Tiny human figures are dwarfed by the dramatic landscape on a hanging scroll from the Ming dynasty. The painter designed this scroll for a friend in exchange for some flower cuttings, and it includes a poem at the top that praises the bright colors of the flowers.

magic and the martial art of kung fu who can turn himself into many different shapes and travel more than 100,000 miles in a single somersault. The Monkey King, a magical pig, and a sea monster all become Xuanzang's followers, and the four of them have many action-packed and funny adventures on their journey. Stories from *The Journey to the West* were performed as plays and puppet-shows, for, just as in Renaissance Europe, more people in Ming China saw performances than read books. Like the plays of Shakespeare, *The Journey to the West* has been turned into movies, children's books, musicals, and comic books, and translated into many languages.

If he returned from the dead, Wu Ch'eng-en might be horrified to learn that his tales of a magical monkey have lasted far longer than his serious Confucian poetry. He would probably not be horrified, or even surprised, however, to know that imperial examinations like the one he took were given in China until the early 20th century. The Ming dynasty collapsed in 1644 much like it had started, with rebel armies attacking the palace of the emperor, but Confucian ideas remained the most powerful force in China for many centuries afterward.

> *Happiness is determined by the thoughts in a person's mind. If he isn't greedy, he can be happy with very little. . . . We are far from having delicious food, yet neither are we suffering from hunger and cold. . . . We do not think of the hardship of the work.*
>
> —Comments of a silk weaver, as told in a story by the Confucian scholar Xu Yikui, about 1390.

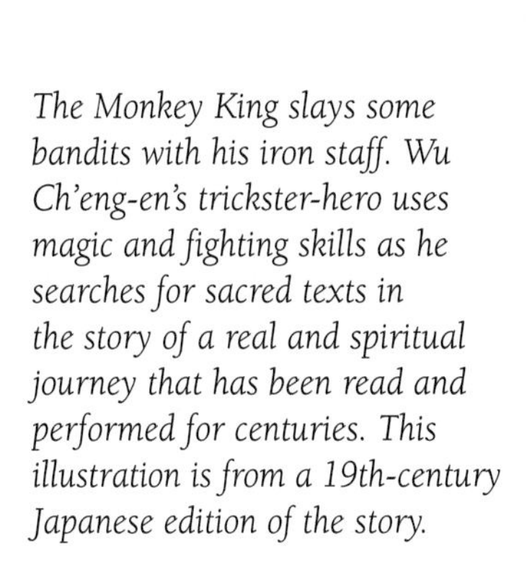

The Monkey King slays some bandits with his iron staff. Wu Ch'eng-en's trickster-hero uses magic and fighting skills as he searches for sacred texts in the story of a real and spiritual journey that has been read and performed for centuries. This illustration is from a 19th-century Japanese edition of the story.

CHAPTER 4

BLACK AND WHITE AND READ ALL OVER

THE PRINTING PRESS

In the middle of the 15th century, Johan Gutenberg, a young man from a wealthy family in the German city of Mainz, learned metalworking from his uncle, who was in charge of a mint where coins were made. Exiled from his home city because of local political squabbles, Gutenberg realized that the metal stamps used to mark goldsmiths' signs on jewelry and fancy tableware could be used for something else. He could cover them with ink and use them to print letters onto paper, in the same way that other craftsmen were using carved wood stamps. These craftsmen carved a whole page in wood, inked it, and pressed it on paper, and then assembled the paper into a book, called a block-book. The carvings could be used only a few dozen times before they became ink-soaked and unreadable, however, and every page of the book required a different carving.

Gutenberg and his assistants made separate stamps—later called type—for every letter of the alphabet, and built racks that held the type in rows. The type could be rearranged for every page and so used over and over. They experimented with different types of ink, discovering that the ink used by artists from Flanders—an area just to the north of Mainz—worked best. Made of oil and lampblack (carbon powder left after burning oil), it clung to the type and didn't drip, then transferred to the writing material cleanly, especially when pressed firmly.

The letters of this modern re-creation of Gutenberg's metal type look backward, but once they are inked and stamped onto paper, they will run correctly left to right. The moveable letters could be used over and over again, so after printing each page, workers in the print shop could reassemble the pieces of type into a new page.

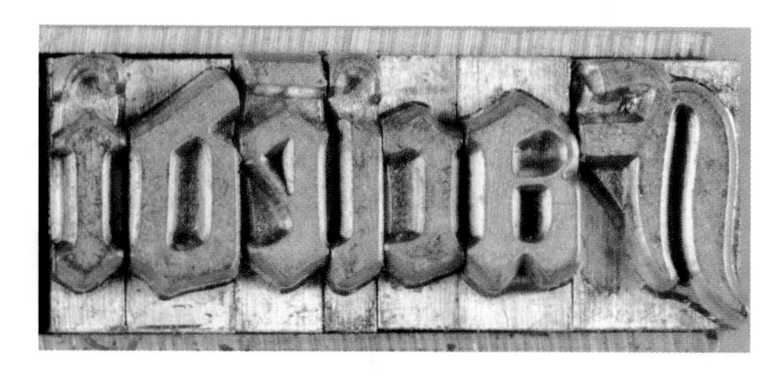

To get that firm, even pressure, racks of type were put into a press, similar to those already used to press grapes for wine, stamp patterns on fabric, or make block-books. The type itself was made by pouring molten metal into molds and

The Gutenberg Museum in Mainz, Germany, put together a reconstruction of Gutenberg's print shop. The tool in the foreground is for applying ink to the type; in the background, printed pages are hung up to dry.

letting it harden, so that when the type got flattened after being pressed many times, it could be melted down, poured back into the molds, and re-made.

By combining existing technologies, Gutenberg invented the printing press with movable metal type, an invention that led to his being ranked number one on a cable-television network's list of "most influential people of the millennium" in 2001. (Five other people discussed in this book also made the top 20: Coming in at number 3 was Martin Luther, then William Shakespeare at 5, Christopher Columbus at 6, Leonardo da Vinci at 11, and Michelangelo at 19.) Why was the printing press so important?

To answer that question, we have to look at what was happening in Europe at the time when Gutenberg lived. After the catastrophe of the Black Death, cities were growing again, and many city people had a little extra money after they had paid for such necessities as food, clothing, and housing. Most of these people could not read, but they saw that learning to read and to do basic arithmetic could bring both practical and spiritual benefits. It could increase the range of jobs open to them and allow them to read the Bible and stories about saints and other holy people. Parents who could not read paid men and women who

A Renaissance schoolmaster advertised for pupils with a painted signboard showing him hard at work. The German text at the top promises that he will teach "young men and young women honestly for a reasonable price."

could to teach their children letters and numbers, and those who could afford it sent their sons to small schools to learn to read Latin.

In Italian cities, the sons of merchants, nobles, or professionals could go to humanist schools to study the classics and learn to speak and write well. Throughout Europe, boys who mastered Latin could go on to one of the many universities—there were about 80 by the end of the 15th century—where they could study to become doctors, lawyers, or university professors. (Women were not allowed to attend universities or become professionals in Europe until the late 19th century, so very few parents arranged for girls to be taught Latin.)

All these groups—children learning letters, boys learning Latin, university students, doctors, lawyers, and adults who wanted to learn new skills or increase their religious understanding—needed material to read. They were already fortunate in one way, because several centuries earlier Europeans had learned how to make paper from the Arabs, who had themselves learned this from the Chinese. Before the adoption of paper, books in Europe had been made out of parchment (stretched sheepskin) or vellum

All the world is full of learned men, of vast libraries... neither in Plato's [the ancient Greek philosopher] time nor in Cicero's [the ancient Roman statesman and author] was there ever such opportunity for study.

—French writer François Rabelais, *Gargantua* (the story of a giant with a huge appetite), 1532 (stretched calfskin), both extremely expensive, especially for large books like the Bible, which took the skins of three hundred sheep.

Paper was made from linen rags and hemp (which came from old rope) shredded in water and mashed until the fibers had broken apart. These fibers were then mixed with more water, and a large, flat wire sieve was dipped into this pulp. The pulp was smoothed over the sieve, the water was pressed out, and the wet sheet of paper was placed on a piece of felt. This whole thing was squeezed in a press (another type of press that Gutenberg adapted for his printing press), hung out to dry, and then often covered with a coating to make it stronger.

Professional copyists writing by hand and block-book makers, along with monks and nuns in monasteries, were already churning out reading materials on paper as fast as they could for the growing number of people who could read. Then Gutenberg developed what he saw at first as a faster way to copy. The earliest printed books looked just like handwritten manuscript books—the letters were very close together, and there were many abbreviations. Copyists used them to speed up their task just like secretaries would later use shorthand to take down spoken conversation or you might use abbreviations when communicating with your friends by e-mail. (R U OK?)

Slowly, printers recognized that they had something quite different: they added more spaces, made letters larger and clearer, and added chapter divisions, more punctuation, tables of contents, and indexes. All this

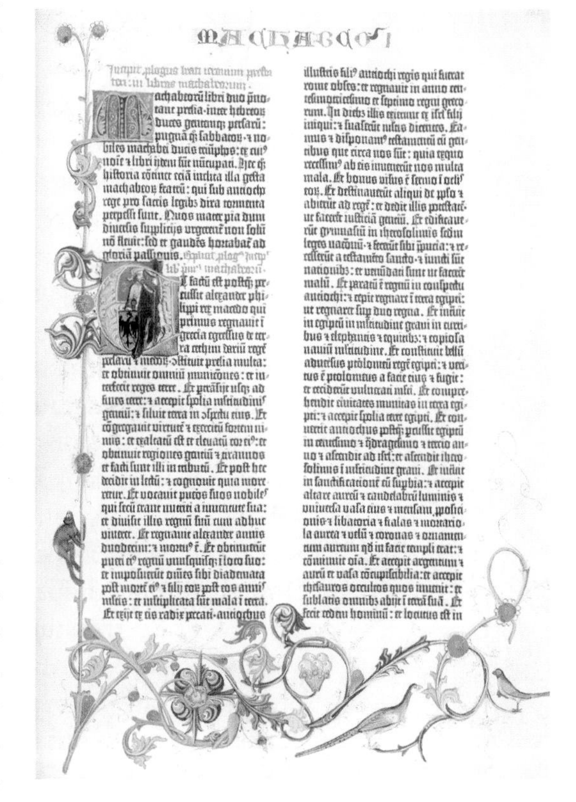

This page from a Gutenberg Bible, printed in 1455, includes hand-painted large letters and decorations in the margins. In this very early printed book, the letters are arranged close together, as they had been in handwritten manuscripts, to save space, and each page was decorated separately by hand.

made printed books easier to read than manuscript books, and they were much cheaper as well. A printer could easily print hundreds or even thousands of copies in the same time that it took a copyist to make just one. As the French poet and scientist Jacques Peletier wrote in the 1560s:

> Ah... one can print in one day
> What it would take thirty days to say
> And a hundred times longer to write in a book.

Gutenberg's invention didn't involve special or secret technology or materials, and he was not the only one to recognize the huge market for books. Soon after Gutenberg began printing, other craftsmen made their own type, built their own presses, and bought their own paper, setting themselves up for business in cities in Germany, Switzerland, and the Netherlands, and then in Italy, England, and France. By 1480, about 110 cities in Europe had presses. Printing continued to spread to Spain and Scandinavia, and by 1500, roughly 50 years after the first books were printed, more than 200 cities and towns in Europe had presses.

The amount of books and other reading material printed was absolutely unbelievable compared with earlier centuries. Historians estimate that somewhere between 8 million and 20 million books were printed in Europe in the 50 years between Gutenberg's invention and 1500. These numbers may seem small compared to today, when the fifth volume in the Harry Potter series sold nearly 7 million copies in one day (making it the fastest-selling book ever), but it was much more than the total number of books produced in all of Western history up to that point. The amounts were so fantastic that some people thought printing was the devil's invention. This opinion did not halt the spread of printing, however, and scholars estimate that by 1600 about 200,000 different books or editions had been printed, with about 1,000 copies each. By this time printing had also spread to the European colonies in the Americas, India, and East Asia.

Ironically, in taking presses to East Asia, Europeans were actually taking them to the place where printing with movable type on paper had first developed. Chinese and

凡欲讀經先念淨口業真言遍
脩唎脩唎 摩訶脩唎 脩脩唎 娑婆訶
奉請除災金剛 奉請辟毒金剛 奉請黃隨求金剛
奉請白淨水金剛 奉請赤聲金剛 奉請定除災金剛
奉請紫賢金剛 奉請大神金剛
金剛般若波羅蜜經
如是我聞一時佛在舍衛國祇樹給孤獨園與大
比丘眾千二百五十人俱爾時世尊食時著衣持
鉢入舍衛大城乞食於其城中次第乞已還至本處
飯食訖收衣鉢洗足已敷座而坐時長老須菩提在大

A Chinese scroll shows the Buddha preaching, along with printed text that includes the date it was made: May 11, 868. This makes it the earliest dated printed book in the world, though Chinese were probably producing block-printed books like this more than 100 years before that.

Koreans had used woodblock printing since at least the 700s, and movable ceramic or wooden type was developed in Korea in the 1200s. Korean printers produced religious works, instructional guides, and laws. They later used metal for making type and the frames that held it in place. We don't know the names of the first Chinese and Korean printers, however, so Gutenberg continues to get the credit. Ts'ai Lun, an official at the court of the Chinese emperor during the late 1st and early 2nd centuries, is usually credited with inventing paper because he was the first person to write about it. However, we have no way of knowing if he actually invented paper or was just the first to describe it.

SAINTS' LIVES AND PRINTER'S DEVILS

What did European printers print? The easiest answer is anything that would sell. They produced matching sets of law books for lawyers, bound in fancy leather; medical manuals and guides to healing herbs for doctors, surgeons, pharmacists, and midwives; grammars and dictionaries for students, often in small sizes with paper covers so that they were cheap and could be carried to class; and books of prayers and sermons for members of the clergy. General readers wanted religious materials; wealthy people bought whole Bibles with decorated leather covers, whereas poorer people bought paperbacks with one or two sermons or a few prayers. People bought these books because they were very interested in religious issues and their own salvation, but also because many religious works were lively, illustrated, and gory. Even books of saints' lives included not only their good deeds and model behavior, but also their violent and tragic deaths. The best-selling book in English for many years was the religious reformer John Foxe's *Book of Martyrs*, which described in gruesome detail the ways in which people were killed for their religious beliefs.

People did not spend all their time reading religious materials, however, and printers recognized very early that there was a market for other types of books and pamphlets. They printed historical romances and biographies of

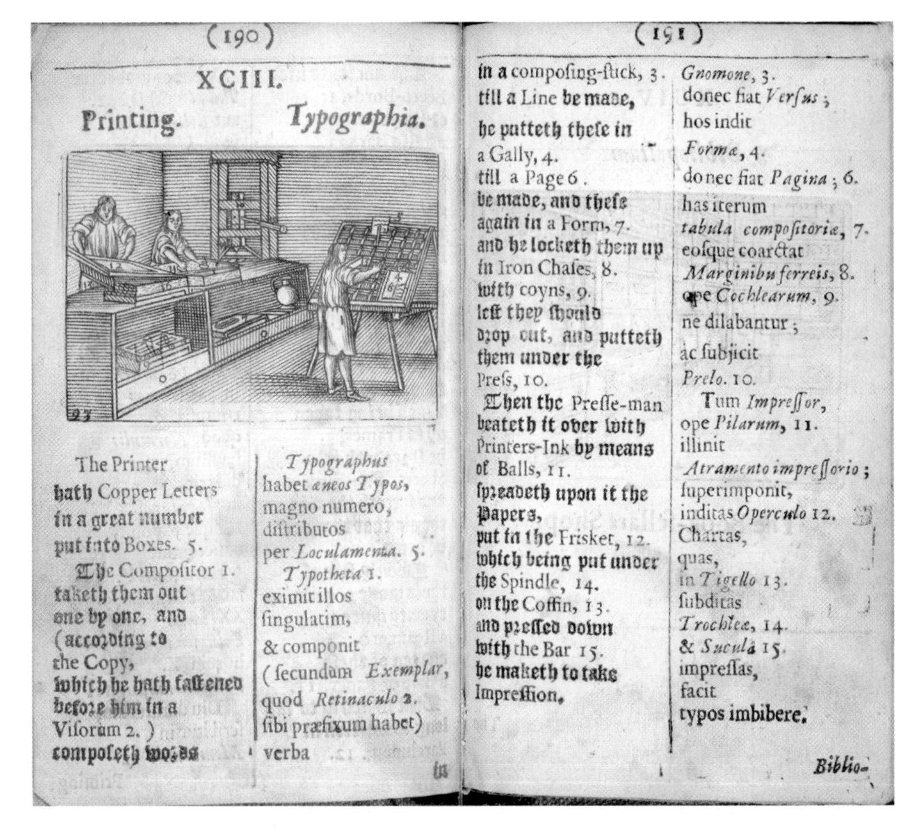

(190)

XCIII.

Printing. *Typographia.*

The Printer
hath Copper Letters
in a great number
put into Boxes. 5.
The Compoſitor 1.
taketh them out
one by one, and
(according to
the Copy,
which he hath faſtened
before him in a
Viſorum 2.)
compoſeth words

Typographus
habet *aeneos Typos,*
magno numero,
diſtributos
per *Loculamenta.* 5.
Typotheta 1.
eximit illos
ſingulatim,
& componit
(ſecundum *Exemplar,*
quod *Retinaculo* 2.
ſibi præfixum habet)
verba

(191)

in a compoſing-ſtick, 3.
till a Line be made,
he putteth theſe in
a Gally, 4.
till a Page 6.
be made, and theſe
again in a Form, 7.
and he locketh them up
in Iron Chaſes, 8.
with coyns, 9.
leſt they ſhould
drop out, and putteth
them under the
Preſs, 10.
Then the Preſſe-man
beateth it over with
Printers-Ink by means
of Balls, 11.
ſpreadeth upon it the
Papers,
put in the Friſket, 12.
which being put under
the Spindle, 14.
on the Coffin, 13.
and preſſed down
with the Bar 15.
he maketh to take
Impreſſion.

Gnomone, 3.
donec fiat *Verſus*;
hos indit
Formæ, 4.
donec fiat *Pagina*; 6.
has iterum
tabula compoſitoriæ, 7.
eoſque coarctat
Marginibus ferreis, 8.
ope *Cochlearum,* 9.
ne dilabantur;
ac ſubjicit
Prelo. 10.
Tum *Impreſſor,*
ope *Pilarum,* 11.
illinit
Atramento impreſſorio;
ſuperimponit,
inditas *Operculo* 12.
Chartas,
quas,
in *Tigello* 13.
ſubditas
Trochleæ, 14.
& *Suculâ* 15.
impreſſas,
facit
typos imbibere.

Biblio-

A 17th-century encyclopedia for children describes the printing process in both Latin and English and includes a labeled diagram. With books like these, young people could learn about the world, and also improve their Latin by using the side-by-side translations.

I wish... the Gospel and the Epistles of Paul... were translated into each and every language... I hope the farmer may sing snatches of Scripture at his plow.

—Dutch humanist Desiderius Erasmus, introduction to his translation of the New Testament, 1512

famous people from the past and present, the more scandalous the better. How-to manuals, such as cookbooks and books of home remedies for everything from headaches to the plague, were very popular. "To preserve your body from the plague," a 16th-century English book advised, heat "a quart of old ale," dissolve in it some "finely powdered ivory" and herbs, and "every morning take five spoonfuls" while "smelling the end of a ship's rope."

There were guides on how to manage your money, how to run a household, and how to write love letters and business letters. There were guides for travelers with handy foreign phrases, discussions of the weather, and descriptions of the strange customs of other lands. After the voyages of discovery, printers found that people liked to read about the experiences of the more adventurous travelers, and they frequently gathered together the most bizarre and exciting travel stories in one volume. Books called bestiaries that told about strange animals and creatures sold very well. Bestiaries described familiar animals such as hedgehogs and porcupines (although telling wild stories about their habits and abilities), exotic animals someone had heard about, such as giraffes or rhinoceroses, and fictitious ones such as centaurs, mermaids, and cyclopes, all mixed in together.

Even though printed books were much less expensive than handwritten ones, they were still fairly costly, so printers also produced smaller, cheaper booklets. These were written in very simple language using a small vocabulary, and often illustrated, so that those who were illiterate or barely literate could also get something from them. Recent

The Only Means of Preserving Our Laws

THOMAS JEFFERSON, LETTER TO GEORGE WYTHE, JANUARY 16, 1796

Sometimes it takes a long time for the full benefits of an invention to be recognized. Several centuries after the development of the printing press, laws in Europe and in Europe's overseas colonies were still not regularly printed, but announced out loud by town criers and government officials riding or walking through the streets. Thomas Jefferson recognized the problems this created, and proposed a solution in a letter written in 1809 to his friend and former teacher George Wythe.

Very early in the course of my researches into the laws of Virginia, I observed that many of them were already lost, and many more on the point of being lost, as existing only in single copies in the hands of careful or curious individuals, on whose deaths they would probably be used for waste paper. I set myself therefore to work to collect all which were then existing.... In searching after these remains, I spared neither time, trouble, nor expense.... But... the question is: What means will be the most effectual for preserving these remains from future loss? All the care I can take of them, will not preserve them from the worm, from the natural decay of the paper, from the accident of fire, or those of removal when it is necessary for any public purpose.... Our experience has proved to us that a single copy, or a few, deposited in manuscript in the public offices cannot be relied on for any great length of time. The ravages of fire and of ferocious enemies have had but too much part in producing the very loss we now deplore. How many of the precious works of antiquity were lost while they existed only in manuscript? Has there ever been one lost since the art of printing has rendered it practicable to multiply and disperse copies? This leads us then to the only means of preserving those remains of our laws now under consideration, that is, a multiplication of printed copies.

battles and their heroes, new tools and techniques, incidents in the lives of famous people, or strange occurrences such as the birth of a two-headed calf or a hailstorm appearing from a cloudless sky were the types of stories printed in these booklets. Especially dramatic events could be publicized in illustrated single sheets called broadsides, which were sold on street corners.

Booklets and broadsides were offered by wandering peddlers who also sold other things such as pins, needles, marbles, and (printed) playing cards, so that printed materials soon showed up in the countryside as well as the cities. Fewer people who lived in rural areas could read than in cities, but a literate person could read a story out loud to friends and family members. The ancient Romans had read everything out loud—fancy houses had special reading rooms where the owner could read without disturbing other people—and many people, even highly educated ones, continued to read aloud as well as silently.

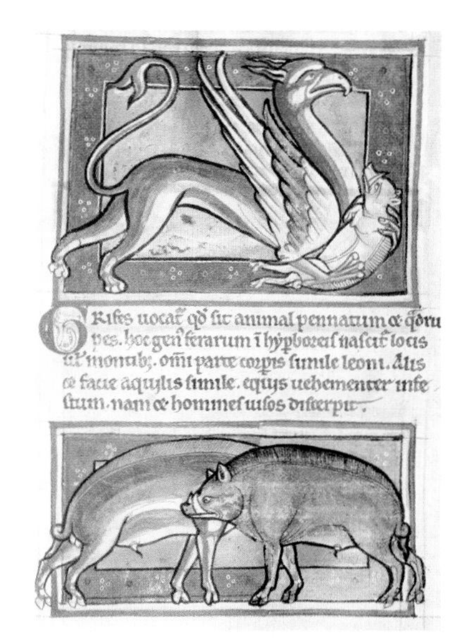

This page from a 12th-century hand-lettered bestiary, or book of strange animals, shows a griffon carrying off a piglet and, at the bottom, two boars. Printers knew that people loved reading bestiaries, so they copied many handwritten ones, keeping them easy to read with large pictures and short text.

The first generation of European printers was made up of men like Gutenberg who were trained in other crafts. But printers soon developed their own organization, called a craft guild, with rules for how workers were to be trained. A boy contracted himself—or his parents contracted him—to a master printer as an apprentice; he worked for five to ten years learning the trade and doing the least skilled and dirtiest tasks. (Other European craftsmen—including butchers, armor-makers, weavers, and many more—also had their own guilds.) Apprentice printers were sometimes called "printer's devils," a name that came either from the fact that they were often black from ink or because they were the scapegoats when something went wrong; printers also spoke about "printer's devils" as spirits that haunted the shop and caused errors.

After his apprenticeship, a young man became what was termed a journeyman, hiring himself out to work for masters for another five to ten years. Then, if he had enough money to establish his own shop, he showed off his skills by printing a complicated work independently. This was called making his "masterpiece," and if it was judged

A 16th-century printer's shop, with men on the right operating the press, women on the left arranging type in racks, and a boy in front—a "printer's devil"—putting pages together. Printer's shops would not normally have been open to the weather; the artist painted the scene in this way to show off his skill with perspective.

acceptable by the other printers, he opened a shop and began hiring his own apprentices and journeymen. Girls were not formally apprenticed in printing, nor in most other trades, but they sometimes learned printing from their fathers or husbands. Women never made masterpieces on their own, but they occasionally ran print shops after being widowed, and their names appear on the title pages of the books they printed just like those of male master-printers. "Being of the female sex did not turn me from the enterprise of publishing," wrote Jeanne Giunta in the French city of Lyon in 1579, "it is not unheard of for women to have such a trade, and obtain thereby the highest of praise."

A printer needed a lot of money for equipment and supplies to make books, and the books he made often took years to sell. Because of this, printers often searched for wealthy patrons who would finance the entire cost of publishing a book. In Venice, humanist nobles interested in Latin and Greek poetry, philosophy, and plays gave money to printers so that they could print fancy editions of important thinkers' works and cheap Greek grammars and dictionaries that would help people learn to read Greek. Merchants who had made money in banking or trade became publishers, sponsoring the printing of certain books but not doing the actual work themselves.

Though they were trained craftsmen, just like bakers or shoemakers, printers had connections to the world of politics, art, and learning that many other craftsmen did not. They depended on local and national governments for jobs. Those governments could also confiscate printed materials they objected to, so printers needed to keep a close watch on politics, or they lost money when they printed banned material. They needed artists to produce woodcuts and engravings to illustrate their major works, and to paint colors and gold dissolved in oil on pictures and letters after these works had been printed.

Printers also needed close and regular contacts with the world of scholarship and learning, and they often hired scholars to check over what they were printing. The Dutch humanist Desiderius Erasmus, who was widely regarded as the most learned man in Europe, began his career as a bishop's assistant and university professor. He decided he was happier with his printer friends, and he spent his later years in their shops, checking his own and others' work for errors, as well as translating and writing. Print shops became gathering places for those interested in new ideas. Some of this atmosphere carried over to early printers' shops in the American colonies, the most well known of which was that of Benjamin Franklin, who began his working life as a printer's devil.

This portrait of the Dutch humanist Desiderius Erasmus shows him surrounded by books as he writes one of his own. The book he is working on sits on a pillow to keep its leather binding from cracking, and Erasmus is dressed in a scholar's robe very similar to those still worn by college and university faculty at graduations today.

A SINGLE INVENTION CHANGES THE WORLD

What effects did this new technology have? Printing gave hundreds or even thousands of people identical books, so that they could discuss the ideas that the books contained with each other in person or through letters. Scientific and scholarly research became a more collaborative effort, with results published quickly, so that the development and spread of ideas was speeded up. Printing strengthened people's imaginations, as they read descriptions of smells, sounds, textures, and landscapes they had not experienced firsthand but conjured up through the words on the page. It also changed their ideas about "facts." Before the spread of printing, people regarded eyewitnesses and personal testimony as more reliable than written documents, because handwritten documents could so easily be forged. Printing made documents appear more trustworthy than people's oral statements or memories because they seemed harder to fake; people now wanted things proved "in black and white," that is, in print.

Learning to read became easier as print was standardized and made clearer, and the number of people who became literate began to grow, especially in the 16th century, when some religious and political leaders supported the opening of elementary schools paid for through taxes. Many people could now afford to own at least a few books. Books freed students from the need for constant memorization, and university lectures were no longer simply someone reading a book aloud. "Why should old men be preferred to their jun-

The power which printing gives us of continually improving and correcting our works in subsequent editions, appears to me the chief advantage of that art.

—Scottish philosopher David Hume, letter to his publisher, 1763 iors now that it is possible for the young by diligent study to acquire the same knowledge?" wrote the Italian humanist Jacobo Foresti in 1483, discussing the hiring of teachers. Because many books were illustrated, some artists became known throughout Europe.

The works of popular authors were sometimes stolen by one printer from another, and then printed in unauthorized editions in the same way that movie DVDs and music CDs are bootlegged today. The religious reformer Martin Luther was the most popular author in Germany during the 16th century; copies of his booklets and books were sometimes stolen as they came off the press, when the master printer wasn't looking, and then published by another printer as well. Authors and printers fumed about this, and gradually the idea of copyright emerged, that is, that people had rights to their words and ideas, and that copying someone else's words was stealing. The notion of copyright later spread to music, art, and commercial slogans and, by the 20th century, to movies, radio shows, audio recordings, and television programs.

The title page of Martin Luther's translation of the Bible into German, published in 1534, has an engraved scene around the margin that was printed along with the written text. This process avoided the slow hand work required for color decorations like those in the Gutenberg Bible. Religious books, including the Bible, were the best sellers of the 16th century.

Government and church leaders all over Europe recognized that a thousand copies of something could influence many more people than just one copy, and they attempted to censor books and authors whose ideas they thought were wrong, usually for political or religious reasons. "The art of printing will so spread knowledge, that the common people, knowing their own rights and liberties, will not be governed by way of oppression," wrote the English philosopher Gabriel Plattes in a political pamphlet in 1641; this is exactly what the rulers of Europe were worried about. Officials developed lists of banned books and authors, enforcing these by confiscating books, arresting printers and booksellers, or destroying the presses of printers who disobeyed. None of this was very effective, and books were printed secretly, with fake title pages, authors, and places of publication, and

Every man should read the Bible, as the very word of God and the spiritual food of man's soul, whereby they may better know their duties to God, to their sovereign lord the king, and their neighbor.

—Bishop Cox's instructions in a speech to people in the English city of Ely, 1571

smuggled all over Europe. By the 17th century, censorship became more effective, and parts of Europe where political and religious authorities did not try to stop the exchange of ideas, such as the Netherlands, became much more important centers of publishing than they had been earlier.

For better or worse, Europe had mass culture for the first time. People in all parts of Europe could hear the same music played from the same printed scores, read the same poets, listen to the same sermons (printers often printed prefabricated sermons for pastors and priests who couldn't come up with their own), make the same dresses (the first printed clothing pattern book was made in 1513), idolize the same kings and ladies, and recognize the same artists. Print brought with it both the chance for greater diversity, because people could learn how others who lived far away thought and acted, and much greater uniformity, as now many thousands of people could come to know exactly the same things. The vast majority of people in Europe during this era were peasant farmers who could not read, and whose information came mostly through hearing and seeing. Nevertheless, even poor villagers might have contact with the world of print through stories or sermons read out loud, or from seeing an illustrated broadsheet about a battle or the appearance of a comet.

The era of the Renaissance and the voyages of discovery saw many new types of technology—cannons and muskets using gunpowder that blew holes in city walls and shot riders off their horses and ships and equipment that allowed seamen to sail out of sight of land on the open waters of the Atlantic and Pacific. In the long run, though, a smaller and quieter invention was probably the most important technical breakthrough: the printing press with movable metal type. In a letter attached to a gift copy of the second book ever printed in France, the printer Guillaume Fichet wrote in 1470, "Bacchus and Ceres [the gods of wine and grain] were made divinities for having taught humanity the use of wine and bread, but Gutenberg's invention is of a higher and diviner order."

CHAPTER 5

LUTHER, LOYOLA, MOBS, AND MASSACRES

THE PROTESTANT AND CATHOLIC REFORMATIONS

"Unless I am convinced of error by the testimony of Scripture and plain reason... I cannot and I will not recant anything, for to go against conscience is neither right nor safe. God help me." These were the words spoken loudly by Martin Luther, a Christian monk and professor of theology at the German University of Wittenberg in 1521. He was standing in front of his monarch, the German Emperor Charles V, and an assembly of government representatives. Luther refused to give in to demands that he take back his harsh criticism of many of the ideas and practices of the church in which he was a monk and go back to obeying the church's leader, the pope in Rome. (The Christian church centered in Rome is usually called Catholic—a word that means worldwide—or Roman Catholic.)

A religious procession winds around the main square of the Italian city of Venice in 1496. Holidays and religious festivals were often marked by processions in which hundreds of people participated, usually walking in groups sorted by occupation.

Other individuals and groups quickly joined in Luther's revolt against the Roman Catholic Church, first in German-speaking parts of Europe and then more widely. Only a few decades after Luther made his statement before the emperor, most of central and northern Europe had split from the church headed by the pope in a movement that came to be called the Protestant Reformation. The label "Protestant" came from "protest," a word used by some of Luther's followers to describe their actions, and "Reformation" from their original goal, which was to reform the church, or make it better, not break away from it.

During the centuries before 1500, the Catholic Church had become a major power in Europe, as well as a religious authority. It owned about one-quarter of the land, and higher officials, including bishops who were in charge of specific regions, and the pope in Rome, often came from noble families and lived in luxury. The pope and some of the bishops were the political rulers of their territories, so they sponsored armies and made and enforced laws just like kings did. Except for Jews in some cities and Muslims in southern Spain and southeastern Europe, all Europeans were officially Christians and paid taxes directly to the church. Some of these taxes went to their local parish priest to support him and keep their church buildings in repair, and some were passed along to the bishops and the pope. People also gave additional money to their local church or to monasteries, where monks and nuns who had made vows of poverty, chastity, and dedication to God lived. In return for these donations, priests, monks, and nuns said special prayers for the soul of the donor or a beloved family member, designed to speed the journey to heaven.

People supported the church financially, but they also did a number of things themselves to help achieve salvation or ask for God's blessing and protection. They learned from their priests and bishops that good works as well as faith were necessary if they were to get into heaven, so they attended church, gave money for the poor, and prayed before eating and sleeping. Processions wound frequently through villages and city streets, honoring Jesus or his mother Mary, or asking a specific saint for a good harvest or prosperity. Expectant mothers prayed to Saint Anne to get through childbirth, women prayed to Saint Sythe to help them find lost keys, parents prayed to Saint Christopher that children be healed from injuries and illnesses, and travelers also prayed to Saint Christopher for protection while on the road. Every stage of life—birth, marriage, and death—was marked by religious rituals. Religious periods and holy days, or holidays as they came to be called, marked the yearly calendar .

Luther was a very dedicated monk who tried to live strictly according to his vows, but he doubted that he could ever be good enough or have faith strong enough to get into heaven on his own merits. He and other Protestant reformers were also not satisfied with many things about the church and about people's religious practices. They thought the pope and bishops had too much power and that, in order to enrich themselves, they led people to believe that donations alone, without faith, would get them into heaven. They believed that many priests, monks, and nuns did not live up to their vows, but instead were worldly and immoral. Protestant reformers criticized the way that church taxes were used, and called for better education for priests so that they would be able to explain Christianity more clearly to ordinary people. They thought that knowing more about Christianity would help people give up practices that the reformers criticized as having no basis in the Bible, such as baptizing magnets to help find lost objects or rubbing a religious object over painful joints or wounds to make them heal.

A reliquary, or relic container, holds the robe of St. Francis of Assisi, one of the patron saints of Italy. Relics are objects associated with the life of Jesus or the saints, often placed into fancy cases, which people purchased for their homes or honored in churches.

The pope, seated on his throne, sells pieces of paper called indulgences that promised to speed people's entry into heaven. Bishops and other eager buyers are lined up in front of him. Woodcuts like this were often printed and sold by artists who wanted to criticize or reform church practices.

None of these criticisms was completely new; people had been calling for reforms in the Catholic Church since the 12th century. The Dutch humanist Desiderius Erasmus published both serious and satirical criticisms, including a short pamphlet titled *Julius Excluded from Heaven,* in which Pope Julius II (the same pope who hired Michelangelo) marches back and forth in front of the gates of heaven, but Saint Peter, who Catholics thought of as the first pope, won't let him in. A few reformers in the centuries before Luther's lifetime began to go even further, however. They said that the pope's supreme authority in the church was not based on the Bible, that the church should give up its wealth, and that the prayers of priests or monks were no more powerful than those of ordinary Christians. The Catholic Church condemned many of these ideas, and executed some people who expressed them, calling them heretics, that is, people whose religious ideas are judged wrong. (Erasmus was not arrested, as he had wisely published *Julius Excluded* anonymously, though people easily guessed who had written it.)

Most people expected that the same thing would happen to Luther. In fact, some of his friends "kidnapped" him for his protection after he made his bold statement to the emperor, spiriting him away to Wartburg Castle in the hills of central Germany, where he remained for almost a year, disguised as a knight. The main reason Luther was not arrested was the political situation in Germany. Germany was not a unified country ruled by a king or queen like France or England, but an empire divided into many small territories, loosely governed by an emperor who was elected by a small group of nobles. The ruler of the territory where Luther lived, called Saxony, was one of these nobles. Though Emperor Charles V made Luther an outlaw in 1521

The Soul Needs Only the Word of God

MARTIN LUTHER, THE FREEDOM OF A CHRISTIAN, 1520

Martin Luther wrote and published many things during his lifetime—formal works on theology (the study of religion), hymns, letters, sermons, political pamphlets, translations of the Old and New Testaments, discussions of current events, and lectures. After he died, his friends and followers even published the comments they remembered him making at dinner, called the "table talk." In 1520, he published a brief pamphlet called The Freedom of a Christian *that summarized his beliefs.*

What can it profit the soul if the body is well, free, and active, and eats, drinks, and does what it pleases? For in these respects even the most godless slave of vice may prosper. On the other hand, how will poor health or imprisonment or hunger or thirst or any other external misfortune harm the soul? Even the most godly men... are afflicted with these things. None of these things touches either the freedom or the servitude of the soul.... One thing, and only one thing, is necessary for Christian life, righteousness, and freedom. That one thing is the most holy Word of God, the gospel of Christ... as the soul needs only the Word of God for its life and righteousness, so it is justified by faith alone and not any works.... But as long as he lives in the flesh... and remains in this mortal life on earth... a man cannot be idle, for his body drives him and he is compelled to do many good works to reduce it to subjection [that is, to make sure his desire for power, money, fame, food, or other earthly things does not take over his life]. Nevertheless the works themselves do not justify him before God, but he does works out of spontaneous love in obedience to God.

These twin portraits of Martin Luther and his wife, Katherina von Bora, were probably painted around the time of their wedding in 1525. Luther taught that almost everyone should marry. His wife was a former nun, and the couple had six children, several of whom died young.

after hearing his speech, and remained a firm supporter of the Catholic Church, he was not willing to order soldiers into Saxony. The pope decreed that Luther was a heretic, but he was more worried about attacks on papal territories by the Ottoman Turks, who had a large army and powerful navy and were expanding their territory in southeastern Europe. Neither the emperor nor the pope moved against Luther, and he spent his year at the Wartburg translating the Bible into German, writing hymns, and deepening his religious ideas.

Others began calling for reform of the Catholic Church, too, and these Protestants all stressed that faith given to believers by God, rather than good works, was the way that people would achieve salvation. They rejected the authority of the pope, and thought that religious services and the Bible should be in the languages people spoke, instead of in Latin, which could only be learned in school. They thought that the Bible alone, not the traditions of the church, was the source for true Christian teachings, and that priests should not have the privileged legal status they did. They believed that no one should take special vows or live in monasteries, but that all Christians, including priests, should get married and live in families, serving God through their work or family life. People should go to church and pray, but pray directly to God or Jesus, not to Mary or the saints, who might have been good people but had no special powers or claim to holiness.

The reformers published their criticisms and ideas using the new technology of the printing press, often in cheap booklets or posters with illustrations showing bishops as wolves or the pope being carried by demons off to hell, so that even people who could not read could easily get the message. In England, William Tyndale, a university scholar like Luther, began to translate the Bible into English in the early 1520s. England was still Catholic and no printer dared publish his Bible, so Tyndale traveled to Germany and found a willing printer. Copies were smuggled back into England, and though the bishop of London burned any he could find, demand for them increased.

Demons drag souls to hell in a cart made out of the body of the pope, with wheels whose spokes are bishops, monks, and cardinals. Religious reformers on all sides often used sermons, pictures, and pamphlets to portray their opponents in very vicious terms.

REFORMS, REVOLTS, AND RIOTS

Why were Protestant ideas attractive? City dwellers objected to the high taxes they had to pay to the church, and to the fact that priests and bishops paid no taxes, so they supported the idea that the church should not have special privileges. In the countryside, peasants liked the emphasis on the Bible and the idea that the clergy were no better than anyone else. In both cities and villages, most people married and had children, so they appreciated the Protestant idea that marriage was just as worthy in God's eyes as vows of chastity. They missed their saints' days and processions, but they replaced these with reading the Bible at home, singing hymns, and listening to much longer sermons in their local languages.

Rulers recognized that breaking with the Catholic Church would allow them to confiscate its land and other property, and give them authority over religion as well as other aspects of life. The rulers of Denmark, Sweden, Norway,

A family kneels in prayer before a crucifix, in a woodcut printed about 1550. Both Protestants and Catholics recommended prayer as an important spiritual activity; the family shown is probably that of the man who paid for this to be printed.

England, Poland, and many of the territories within the German empire accepted Protestant religious ideas, fully understanding the practical benefits, and became Protestant.

Whether rulers became Protestant or remained Catholic, they expected that everyone in their territory would follow their example. Most people agreed with their rulers that there should be just one official church in any country, but a few people thought that allegiance to a particular version of Christianity should be voluntary. As a symbol of this voluntary commitment, they supported baptism for adults who could decide their religion for themselves, rather than for infants. They broke with Catholic ideas even more than Luther had, and often attempted to follow Christ's teachings as given in the Bible to the letter. Because they wanted a very sharp break with the past, people who had such ideas were called radicals.

Because radical Christians often took the words of the Bible literally, many of them were pacifists, refusing to fight in wars because the Bible says "turn the other cheek." "It is written" said the radical reformer Michael Sattler, speaking at his trial in 1527, shortly before he was executed for his religious ideas, "Thou shalt not kill. We must not defend ourselves against our persecutors, but repel and resist them with earnest prayer to God." The Bible also teaches that "it is easier for a camel to pass through the eye of a needle than for a rich man to get into heaven," so some radical groups opposed all differences in wealth, and owned all their property in common. These religious ideas appealed to people who wanted to make changes in society, such as poor peasants and townspeople, and sometimes led to violent riots and revolts against wealthy landlords or churches.

Catholics and most Protestants, including Luther, opposed the radicals' ideas and actions, and many thousands of radicals were persecuted, tortured, and executed, sometimes in very gruesome ways. "After she had borne that child in torment," sang a Dutch hymn about a pregnant woman who was arrested and tortured, "they threw her into the Scheldt," a nearby river. Her husband, sang the hymn, had earlier gone "to the stake" to be burned, but "had no fear." Radical groups fled from one part of Europe to another, and many of them, such as the Quakers, Unitarians, Amish, and Mennonites, eventually went to North America, where the idea that church and state should be separate became part of the U.S. Constitution.

Radicals were not the only people who met with violence. Both Catholic and Protestant rulers often forbade people from Christian groups other than their own to worship, and sometimes arrested and killed them. William Tyndale was executed, along with other Protestants, by authorities in the Netherlands, where the Catholic emperor Charles V was the ruler. This persecution led people to migrate to places where their religious ideas matched those of the rulers, leaving their homes and property behind. Religious wars brought further violence and disruption.

At the same time that they were hunting down their religious opponents, authorities also rounded up, tried, and often executed people for witchcraft. Most people regarded witchcraft—in which, they thought, the accused person made a pact with the devil to do his bidding—as a sinister and widespread threat. Printed pamphlets fueled the hysteria, reporting on witches who "killed nineteen children and three expectant mothers" and "danced in a circle with the devil." Most of the people accused of witchcraft were women, some of whom did in fact believe they were witches.

We are ready to suffer and to await what God is planning to do with us. . . . We will continue in our faith in Christ so long as we have breath in us.

—Michael Sattler, words spoken at the trial that ended with his execution, 1527

However, these women were usually guilty of no more than muttering curses when they were angry or being around children or animals that happened to get sick or die.

By the 1550s, the Protestant Reformation had developed beyond the ideas of Luther. John Calvin, who had trained as a lawyer, inspired the most dynamic form of Protestantism. Calvin was born and educated in France, but fled to Switzerland when he became a Protestant. There he used his legal training in reasoning to take Protestant ideas to what he saw as their logical outcome. If God is all-powerful and human faith comes from God, Calvin reasoned, then there is no free will, that is, people cannot decide on their own whether they will have faith. All humans are naturally sinful and on their own merits would go to hell, but instead, wrote Calvin in the *Institutes of the Christian Religion* in 1559, God "in his freely given mercy, without regard for human worth" decrees "eternal life for some, eternal damnation for others." A person's own actions can do nothing to change this "terrible eternal decree," an idea Calvin called predestination.

One of John Calvin's students doodled a sketch of his professor during a lecture. As the drawing suggests, Calvin was a reserved man who did not reveal his emotions easily.

Though you might think that this would be a very depressing idea and would lead people to just do whatever they wanted, it actually had the opposite effect. Calvinists came to believe that hard work, thrift, and proper moral conduct were signs that you were among the "elect," or the special people, chosen for salvation. Business or personal success were taken as further signs of salvation. Merchants and craftsmen in prosperous cities were attracted to Calvinism because of the sense of purpose it offered.

Calvin first put his ideas into action in the Swiss city of Geneva, after the city leaders invited him in to reform the government. He established a special court for investigating and disciplining people accused of drunkenness, profanity, gambling, family or neighborhood fights, following different religious ideas, or not going to church. Under Calvin's leadership, the city forbade dice and card games, dances, and plays, and even tried to close the taverns, though this last effort wasn't very successful. City authorities questioned people about what was going on in their neighborhoods, and encouraged children to report suspicious or improper activities of older family members. Calvin set up an academy for training pastors, and these young men spread Calvinist ideas into France, the Netherlands, Germany, England, Scotland, Hungary, and Poland. In some parts of Europe, Calvinists published pamphlets calling for people to resist the power of rulers they judged "ungodly." These pamphlets later came to influence writers urging the overthrow of monarchs judged to be "unjust," including supporters of the American Revolution.

What in us seems perfection itself corresponds ill to the purity of God. . . . Man is never sufficiently touched or affected by the awareness of his lowly state until he has compared himself with God's majesty.

—John Calvin, *Institutes of the Christian Religion*, 1559

ONE GOOD REFORMATION DESERVES ANOTHER

The successes of Calvinism spurred the Catholic Church into a more vigorous response to Protestant challenges. The popes themselves became reformers, forbidding men to buy positions as bishops; reducing their own expenses on fancy furniture, food, and art; and making other changes. Popes also supported measures to combat the spread of Protestant teachings. They organized a special court, called the Inquisition, that investigated people suspected of having opinions unacceptable to the Catholic Church, and set up the Papal Index, a list of authors and books that people were forbidden to print, sell, or read. They called church leaders to a meeting at Trent, on the border between Italy and Switzerland. The Council of Trent stated clearly, in opposition to Protestant beliefs, that good works as well as faith are necessary for salvation; that the traditions of the church as well as the Bible contain essential Christian teachings; that priests are different from anyone else because they have special powers in church rituals, and they are not to marry; and that the Virgin Mary and the saints should be honored.

Along with reform-minded popes, new groups within the clergy, especially the Society of Jesus, or Jesuits, were

Ignatius Loyola, dressed as a knight in the black armor common in Spain, carries a lance. This portrait by an unknown French admirer captures Loyola's military background and strong sense of purpose.

major forces in the Catholic Reformation. The Jesuits were founded by a Spanish knight, Ignatius Loyola, who had dreamed about adventure after reading books about the daring exploits of legendary fighters. Loyola was badly wounded in a battle, and during the many horribly painful months it took for his shattered leg to heal, he read books about saints and martyrs that happened to be available. His reading made him decide to give up his life as a soldier, and put his military discipline and training in service to the pope and the Catholic Church instead. "Just as taking a walk, journeying on foot, and running are bodily exercises, so we call spiritual exercises every way of preparing the soul to seek and find the will of God," he wrote in the *Spiritual Exercises,* a sort of how-to manual published in 1548 for those who wanted to serve God. Loyola's charismatic personality and tremendous energy attracted other dedicated young men, and in 1540 he and his followers formed a new group to carry out action on behalf of the Catholic Church, the Society of Jesus.

The Jesuits set up schools, taught at universities, preached popular sermons, and worked as missionaries. In Europe, they were very effective at stopping the further spread of Protestant ideas, and even reconverted some areas, such as Poland, back to Catholicism. Jesuit missionaries traveled to places far beyond Europe, including European colonies in Brazil, Mexico, India, and Japan, where they worked to convert local people to Christianity.

Man is created to praise, reverence, and serve God our Lord, and by this means to save his soul. . . . Therefore, we must make ourselves indifferent to all created things.

—Ignatius Loyola, *The Spiritual Exercises*, 1548

The achievements of the Jesuits made many women eager to found a similar group, but church leaders were horrified at the idea of women out in public preaching and teaching. They encouraged women instead to pray for Catholic successes, from their homes if they were married and from behind the walls of their convents if they were nuns. Teresa of Avila, a Spanish nun whose prayers brought her visions of God, chose to see this encouragement as a call to action. "The Lord walks among the pots and pans," she wrote in *The Way of Perfection* during the 1560s. "If we can obtain some answers from God to our prayers, we shall be fighting for Him even though we are very cloistered [that is, shut inside a convent]." Teresa used her tremendous energy to travel around Spain reforming and reorganizing women's convents—in a letter written in 1576, one church official called her "a restless, disobedient and obstinate woman." Other women were even bolder, setting up convents in places where European countries were establishing colonies, such as Mexico, Peru, the Philippines, and later French Canada.

The Reformation also brought with it more than a century of religious wars in Europe. In France, Calvinists and Catholics grew ever more intolerant of each other, with each side calling the other "poisoners" and "blasphemers," who would provoke God's anger. Mobs on both sides killed their opponents, and in 1572 thousands of Protestants were slaughtered on one day in a massacre secretly organized by some of the Catholic king's advisors. This led to open warfare, further riots, and assassinations, until finally in 1598 the new king of France declared a truce, stating that France was officially Catholic but Protestants would be able to live, work, and worship freely in some areas.

In the Netherlands, Calvinists revolted against the Catholic king of Spain, who also ruled the Netherlands. Protestant ideas taught people to reject the power of sacred images, and mobs in many cities took down and smashed statues, stained-glass windows, and paintings. They ridiculed religious images, throwing paintings into latrines, using wooden crucifixes as firewood, or giving statues of saints to children as toys. A brutal general brought mob vio-

Catholic missionaries used drawings to teach Christian beliefs to Native Americans and other potential converts around the world. This page from a catechism—a short book explaining basic beliefs—shows, at the left of the second row, the Holy Spirit coming to the kneeling Virgin Mary, and, at the bottom right, Christ, dressed as a knight and carrying a flag, rising from the dead.

lence to a head with a bloody reign of terror called the "Council of Blood," which executed thousands of people.

Like the civil war in France, the struggle in the Netherlands dragged on for many years, and the Protestants looked for allies. Queen Elizabeth I of England, who was Protestant, reluctantly sent some money and troops, which led King Philip II of Spain to plan an invasion of England. The Armada—the Spanish word for "fleet"—left Spain a year later than planned because English pirates (with Elizabeth's

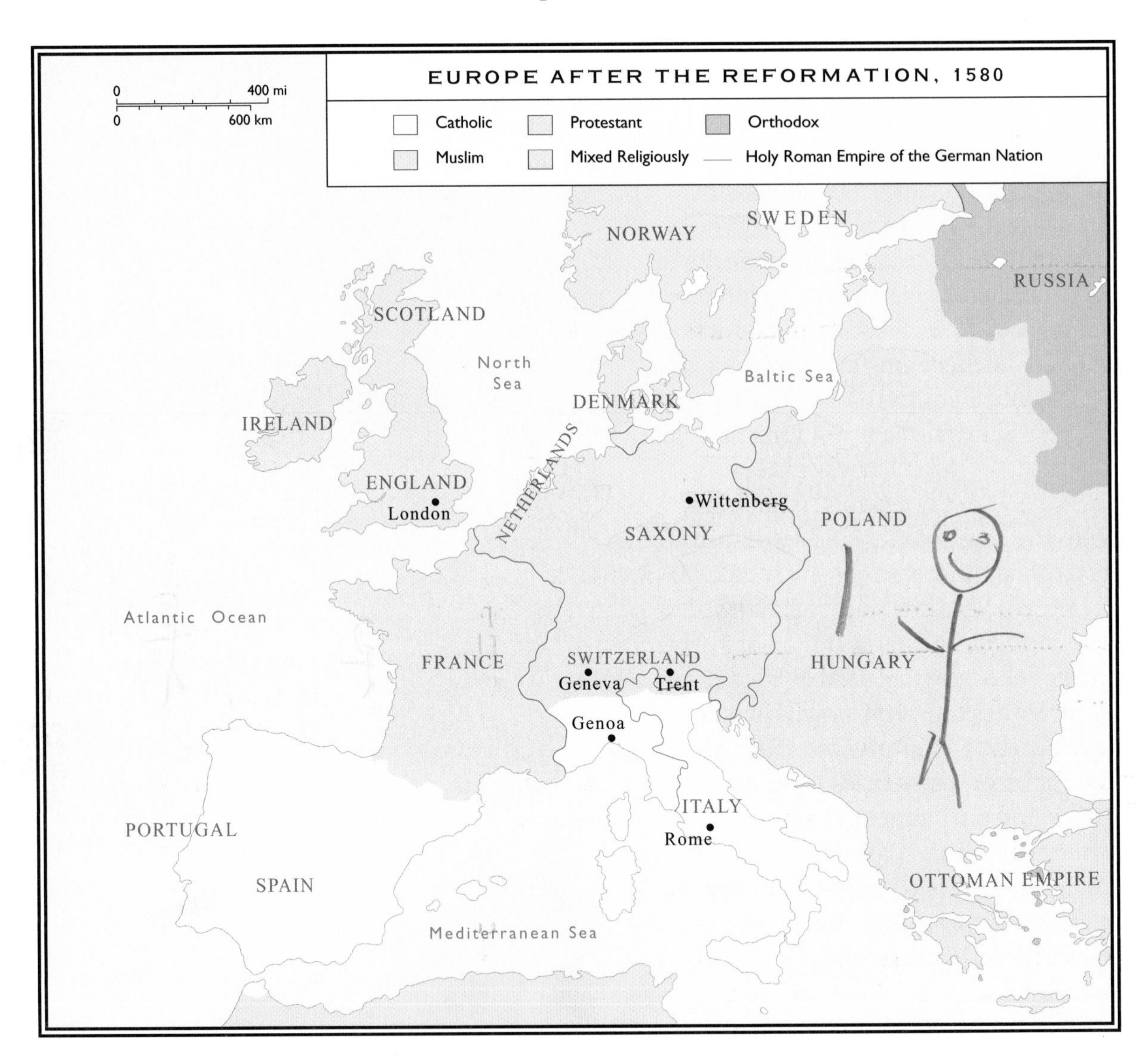

Calvinists in the Netherlands pull down statues and break stained-glass windows in a Catholic church. Calvinists believed that religious images distracted people from worshipping God properly, so they removed them from churches or destroyed them.

blessing) had burned most of the Spaniards' barrels for food and water as they lay stacked on the docks, and new ones had to be built. The Armada finally left Spain with about 130 ships, and the pope's blessing, in 1588. It was a disaster.

The Spanish ships were less maneuverable than the English ones, so they couldn't get close enough to fire on their enemy. Shifting winds and fireships (unmanned, burning ships used to set fire to enemy vessels) launched by sailors from England and the Netherlands scattered the Spanish ships, many of which sailed right past England into the North Sea. The new barrels leaked, many of the Spanish sea captains didn't have enough experience, and Philip's plans were never communicated clearly. Some of the ships did straggle back to Spanish ports, but Philip never ordered another invasion. In 1609, Spain agreed to a truce, dividing the Netherlands into a Catholic part still ruled by Spain (now Belgium) and an independent Protestant part (now the Netherlands).

The religious reform that Luther had started permanently changed the world in ways he never intended. Western Europe remained religiously divided from that point on, and the divisions were carried to the rest of the world by missionaries and colonists.

Nor did You, Lord, when You walked in the world, despise women; rather, You always, with great compassion helped them . . . these are times in which it would be wrong to undervalue virtuous and strong souls, even though they are women.

—Saint Teresa of Avila, *The Way of Perfection*, 1560s

CHAPTER 6

"ASTONISHING," "MAGNIFICENT," "GREAT"

RULERS AND RELIGION IN EUROPE AND ASIA

Forty years after Pope Julius II and Michelangelo fought over the speed with which the artist was completing the Sistine Chapel paintings, another brilliant artist and his domineering patron were having a similar fight. In the 1550s, Suleyman, the sultan (a word meaning "ruler") of the Ottoman Empire, hired Mimar (a word meaning "architect" in Turkish) Sinan to design and build a vast religious complex in Istanbul, called the *Suleymaniye*. Work had been delayed, and rumors spread to the sultan that the architect was incompetent and that the main dome of the central mosque was ready to collapse. In a rage, Suleyman stormed to the building site and threatened to throw the architect in prison.

The domed Suleymaniye mosque in Istanbul, with its tower-like minarets from which chanters called people to prayer, was designed by Mimar Sinan and built between 1550 and 1557 by Sultan Suleyman. The mosque sits in the middle of a large palace compound, also designed by Sinan, with schools, hospitals, shops, and places for travelers to stay.

Mimar Sinan responded by promising that the mosque would be finished in two months, a promise that everyone at the sultan's court thought was insane. Sinan stuck to his promise, and two months later the mosque was done, with a central dome that was perfectly fine. A century later, an Ottoman chronicler reported the amazement of some Christian visitors to the Suleymaniye, "When they beheld the dome they tossed up their hats and cried Maria! Maria! And on observing the four arches supporting the dome... they could not find terms to express their admiration." They were equally struck by the slender towers, or minarets, outside the domed mosque, for "each bit his finger from astonishment." Mimar Sinan went on to design and build many more mosques, schools, palaces, and other buildings, outliving Sultan Suleyman by more than 20 years.

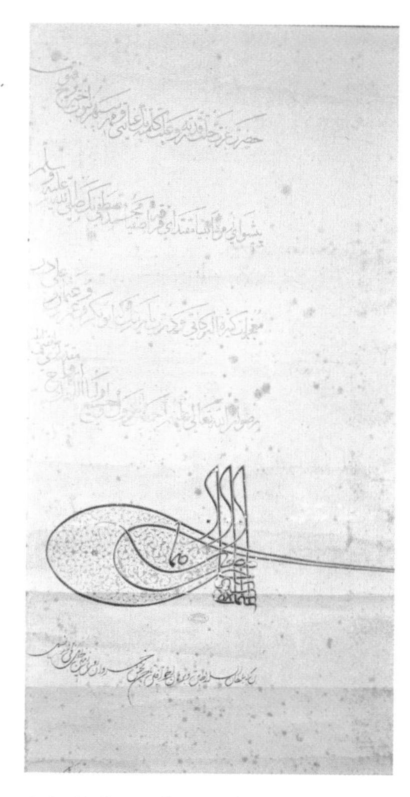

A 1528 letter from Sultan Suleyman to King Francis I of France ends with the sultan's elaborate and decorative signature. Francis had asked Suleyman to turn a mosque in Jerusalem—which was then part of the Ottoman Empire—into a Christian church. In this letter Suleyman answered that he was pleased about the growing friendship between their two countries (though we don't know if he did turn the mosque into a church).

Reactions like those of the visitors to the mosque led Sultan Suleyman to be known in Europe as "the Magnificent" —the same title given to Michelangelo's patron Lorenzo de' Medici. The title his own people gave him was Suleyman the Lawgiver, because of the many laws he issued during his long reign. Support for religion, patronage of the arts, and expansion of the legal system were just some of the things that made Suleyman's reign later appear to be the "golden age" of the Ottoman Empire. At the same time that Protestant and Catholic Christians in western Europe were fighting each other in religious wars, Suleyman and other rulers of the Ottoman Empire decided on a different way to handle religious differences. They figured that tolerating religious differences would help keep different groups more satisfied with their rule than trying to force all their subjects to adopt the same religion.

If that didn't work, however, they had no problem using force, and they made effective use of new types of weapons, especially those that used gunpowder. For that reason, the Ottoman Empire is sometimes called a gunpowder empire. A well-organized bureaucracy, prosperous trade relationships, public works projects such as schools and hospitals, and government support for literature, the arts, and religion were just as important as gunpowder, however, in helping the Ottoman sultans maintain power and wealth.

The word "Ottoman" comes from the name of Osman Bey, the capable leader of a group of Turks who began to expand their territory in modern-day Turkey in the 13th century. Ottoman forces entered Europe in 1345, and by 1550 they ruled an empire that stretched from Egypt in the south to Serbia in the north to Iraq in the east. They required conquered peoples to pay taxes, but allowed them to keep their own laws and traditions, including their religion. The Ottoman sultans were Muslim, but, in contrast to the rulers of Europe, they did not think it was important that all their subjects followed the same religion. In fact, because non-Muslims had to pay higher taxes, the sultans were not eager to have their subjects convert.

Muslims regarded Christians and Jews as fellow "Peoples of the Book," because all three religions were based on divine revelations from a god that Muslims understood to be the same. ("Allah" is the Arabic word for "God.") In some parts of the Muslim world, life was difficult for Christians and Jews, but within the Ottoman Empire they

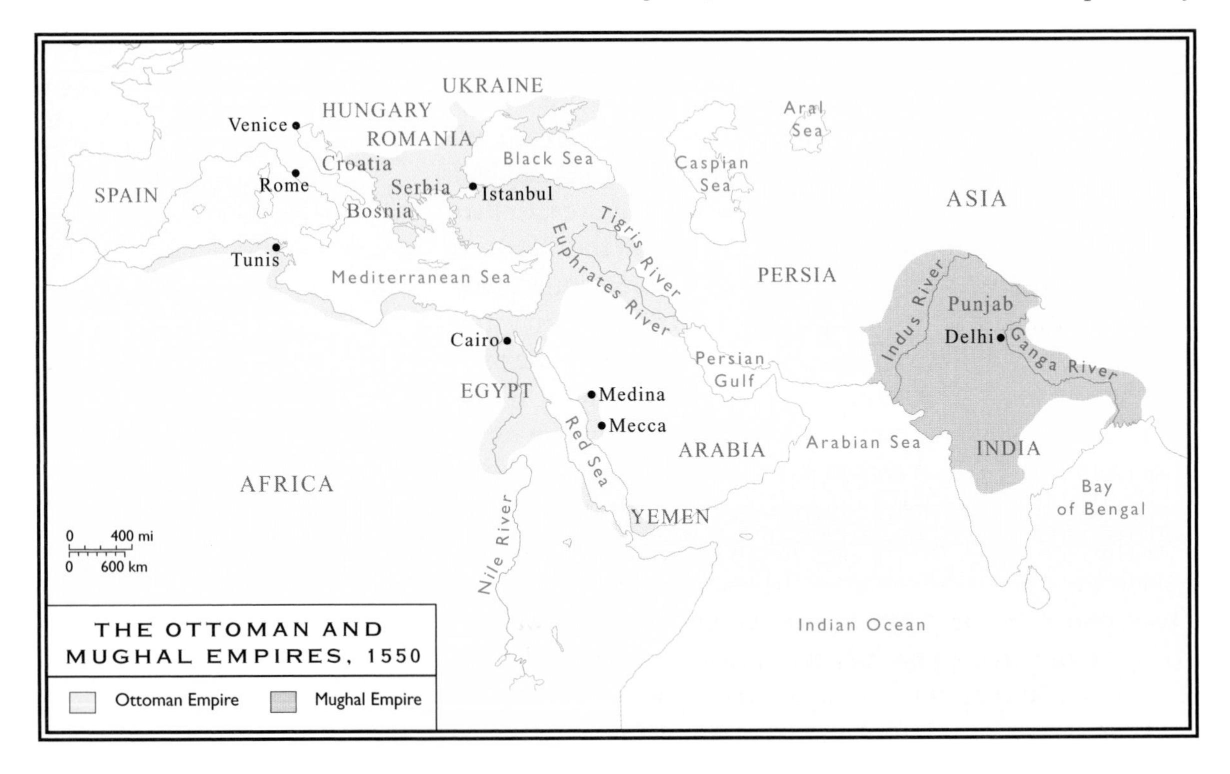

could practice their religion openly. They could keep their own systems of religious law, control family matters such as marriage, and teach their children religious ideas and traditions. Christian and Jewish leaders often held high offices at the sultan's court. Less than half the Ottoman Empire was Muslim in the 16th century, though slowly more and more people converted.

This acceptance of religious diversity was very different from the ideas of most Christian monarchs in Europe, and especially the rulers of the states at the other end of the Mediterranean Sea from the Ottomans, in what would become Spain. Muslim troops had conquered most of the area that is now Spain in the eighth century, building the magnificent city of Córdoba as their capital. Gradually, however, Christian armies from the north conquered Muslim forces, and set up several small kingdoms. By the late 1200s, the Muslims only held the small kingdom of Granada in the south, though some people in other parts of Spain continued to practice Islam, as they had for centuries.

Around 1300, Jews were expelled from England and France, because the rulers of those countries wanted their money. The rulers found it easy to make Christians suspicious of a group whose religious practices were so different from their own, and with the help of hostile Christians they were able to force the Jews to flee, leaving their money and property behind. Many Jews settled in the Muslim and Christian parts of Spain. At first the rulers of both faiths welcomed them, but by about 1400 Jews in Christian areas were attacked, and many of them converted to Christianity.

No distinction is attached to birth among the Turks... it is by merit that men rise in the service, a system which ensures that positions should only be assigned to the competent... with us there is no opening left for merit... the prestige of birth is the sole key to advancement.

—Ogier Ghislein de Busbecq, ambassador from the German emperor to the court of Suleyman the Magnificent, letter to the emperor, 1560

JEWISH SCAPEGOATS AND CHRISTIAN SOLDIERS

Why did Christians in Europe hate Jews? In many parts of Europe, Jews were forbidden to own land, so they turned to trade and banking to support themselves. Rulers who wanted to expand the economy of their territory encouraged Jews to settle in growing cities. These rulers gave Jews special privileges, which made people resent them, and also made

When King Ferdinand of Aragon and Queen Isabella of Castile got married, their two countries were united to form Spain. This portrait was part of a book of prayers made for their daughter, and it emphasizes their Catholic faith by showing them with a saint holding a cross.

them vulnerable, because they were dependent on the whims of the ruler. If the rulers decided that they wanted Jewish property, they just took it and ordered the Jews out. They justified their actions by repeating rumors about the Jews. Jews "go down secretly into underground vaults and kill a Christian as a sort of sacrifice," wrote a Christian monk in 1186, in a chronicle about a French king. "Inspired by the devil," he continued, they "scorned the Christian religion," and used the blood of Christian children for their religious rituals. None of these accusations was true, but they fueled Christian hatred and led to the killing of Jewish families and communities, especially during times of turmoil such as the Black Death.

In 1469, Princess Isabella of Castile, the heiress to one of the Christian kingdoms in Spain, married Prince Ferdinand of Aragon, the heir to another, and the kingdoms were slowly united. Ferdinand and Isabella, but especially Isabella, believed they had a mission to promote Christianity by converting or banishing all Muslims and Jews, and making sure all Christians were pure in their faith. They got the permission of the pope, who declared them "Their Most Catholic Majesties," to set up an Inquisition, or trial, controlled by men they appointed, to enforce Christian beliefs. (This was separate from the inquisition controlled directly by the pope, though it had the same goals.) With secret trials, the use of torture, and public punishments, the Spanish Inquisition investigated Christian converts suspected of not having really given up their Jewish or Muslim beliefs. After the Reformation, they also tried people suspected of being Protestant. Trials and executions of converts began immediately, with jealousy and resentment leading people to testify against their neighbors.

Ferdinand and Isabella sent armies against Granada, which they conquered in 1492. That same year they ordered all Jews who had not converted to leave Spain, and perhaps as many as 200,000 left. They "sold their houses, their landed estates, and their cattle for very small prices," wrote a Jewish chronicler in 1495, and "many of them died in the fields from hunger, thirst, and lack of everything." Many went to the Ottoman Empire, where the sultan "received them kindly, as they were craftsmen," and he needed their skills. Ten years later, Muslims who had not converted were also ordered to leave, and some went to the Ottoman Empire.

The Ottoman sultans clearly benefited from their policy of religious toleration, but their tolerance was limited by their need for soldiers. Prisoners of war and convicts were used as military slaves in many armies throughout the world. In the 15th century the sultans began to require their Christian subjects to supply a certain number of young boys from each village along with their taxes. These boys, called Janissaries from the Turkish *yeni cheri* (meaning "new troops") were raised in Turkish foster homes, learned the Turkish language, converted to Islam, and received extensive military training. They fought alongside Turkish troops and were often the first to use new types of weapons. Janissaries were legally slaves of the sultan, but they could gain power and prestige through their service. The most capable became senior officials and ambassadors as well as admirals and generals, and the very best could hold the highest office of grand vizier, second only to the sultan.

In the early 16th century, Ottoman armies under the leadership of Sultan Selim "the Grim" took over the entire eastern Mediterranean, Egypt, North Africa, and the Arabian Peninsula. This territory included all the holy places of Islam. To reinforce their religious authority, the Ottomans moved the Caliph of Cairo, Egypt, the head of the branch of Islam called Sunni, to Istanbul. Under Selim's son, Suleyman the Magnificent, Ottoman troops conquered Bosnia, Croatia, Romania, the Ukraine, and much of Hungary; fought naval battles against the ships of the Italian cities Venice and Genoa; and defeated the armies of other

We order all Jews and Jewesses of whatever age they may be, who live, reside, and exist in our said kingdoms... that by the end of the month of July, they depart from all of these our said realms... and they shall not dare to return to those places, [under] penalty of death and the confiscation of all their possessions.... And we command and forbid that any person or persons of the said kingdoms, shall dare to receive, protect, defend, nor hold publicly or secretly any Jew or Jewess... under pain of losing all their possessions.

—Decree of Ferdinand and Isabella expelling the Jews from Spain, March 30, 1492

Janissaries ride expensive horses and wear fancy uniforms and elaborate hats. Janissaries were elite troops trained to fight for the sultans of the Ottoman Empire. They were originally taken as young boys from Christian families, but by the 17th century they were recruited from Muslim families as well.

Muslim empires in present-day Iraq. These conquests left the Ottomans as the rulers of about a third of Europe and half of the Mediterranean shoreline for the next three hundred years.

THE TIGER AND HIS TOLERANT GRANDSON

At just about the same time as Suleyman's conquests, another Muslim ruler, Zahir al-Din Muhammad, who became known as Babur (the Persian word for "Tiger"), was conquering northern India and establishing the Mughal Empire. Babur was a central Asian ruler who claimed to be descended from two earlier Mongol conquerors, Genghis Khan and Tamerlane. ("Mughal" is the Persian word for Mongol). In 1526, using artillery and handheld firearms, Babur's small invasion force defeated the sultan of Delhi, and went on to conquer much of northern India. His grandson Akbar (a name that means "greater than anything else") took over the throne when he was only 13. He was a very effective warrior and military leader, and his empire grew to cover two-thirds of South Asia, including most of present-day Afghanistan, Pakistan, north and central India, and Bangladesh. Both Babur and Akbar outfitted their forces with new types of weapons, so the Mughal Empire is also called a gunpowder empire.

Akbar's parents came from two different branches of the Muslim faith, and Akbar appointed officials from both of these branches. He also appointed followers of Hinduism, the religion of most Indian people. Akbar won support from Hindu leaders, especially the powerful Rajputs, the former rulers of a kingdom in northern India, by making them administrators and military commanders. Just like the Ottoman rulers, Akbar let his subjects follow their own laws and customs: Hindus followed Hindu law, and Muslims followed Muslim law.

A Mughal battalion stages an attack in this battle scene from the Baburnama, *the memoirs of the Mughal emperor Babur. Mounted troops and foot soldiers wielding swords lead the attack. On the rock outcroppings at the upper left are cannons whose smoke and noise would have helped to disrupt enemy lines.*

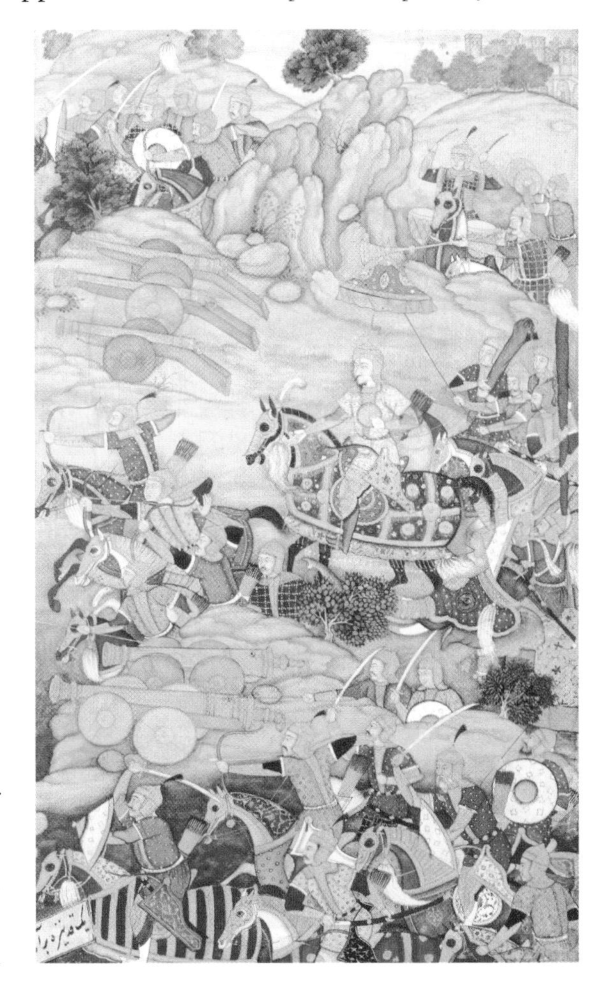

Akbar's toleration of religious differences went beyond that of the Ottomans, and was not motivated simply by practical issues. He thought that bringing religions together would promote justice and harmony, and also increase support for his rule. He married a princess from a Rajput family, so that his children would have both Hindu and Muslim ancestry. He built a special building where scholars from various religions could discuss their beliefs and practices.

Most of the people in India were Hindu, a very old religion practiced in India for thousands of years. Hinduism was (and still is) very diverse. Groups varied in their forms of worship, beliefs about the gods and goddesses, festivals, saints, rituals, and shrines. All Hindus share a group of sacred writings, believe in one universal divine spirit and that

Most of the inhabitants of India are infidels, believing mainly in the transmigration of souls; all artisans, wage-earners and officials are Hindus. . . . Every artisan follows the trade handed down to him from his forefathers.

—The Mughal conqueror Babur, *The Baburnama,* 1520s

the soul is reborn after the body dies (called reincarnation), and accept the caste system, a strict order of social classes determined by birth. Caste and reincarnation are linked. If a person lives a good life, the soul will be reborn into a higher state, perhaps into the body of a person of higher caste. If a person leads an evil life, the soul will be born into a lower state, either a lower-caste person or even an animal. According to this belief, animals have souls, which is why Hindus are often vegetarians or consider certain animals sacred. The process of reincarnation can continue for thousands of years, although souls can ultimately reach a state of spiritual perfection from which they never return.

Along with Hinduism and Islam, people followed many other religions in the Mughal Empire of Akbar's day. On the southwest coast of India, there were well-organized Christian churches that dated back to the fifth century or perhaps even earlier. There were Jews in many Indian cities. There were Zoroastrians, followers of an ancient Persian religious leader who taught that the world is a battle between the forces of good and evil. Indian Zoroastrians were called Parsis (which means "Persians" in Hindi, one of the languages spoken in India), and believed that each person would be judged on how well he or she had stood up for the forces of good.

The Mughal emperor Akbar died not long after this portrait was sketched. Akbar promoted religious tolerance and greatly increased the size of the Mughal Empire, but his later life brought family problems, which might be the reason he seems to be deep in thought.

Along with religions that were brought into India, there were religions that developed internally. Jainism was founded in India in the 500s BCE by a religious reformer named Mahavira, a name that means "The Great Hero." Jains believed (and continue to believe) that all life is sacred because every physical body contains an eternal soul. Most were strict vegetarians, and many worked in trade or other businesses rather than growing crops and raising chickens and goats, so that they did not have to kill any living things.

The Sikh religion was founded by Shri Guru Nanak Devi Ji, a religious teacher who lived in the Punjab area of what is now along the border between India and Pakistan. The word Sikh means "learner." Nanak was born into a higher-caste Hindu family, and even as a teenager spent more time meditating than his parents wanted him to. In 1507, Nanak received a religious vision that he later turned into the basic Sikh statement of faith, "There is but One God, His name is Truth, He is the Creator, He fears none, He is without hate." Nanak traveled with a low-status Muslim musician, and often ate with lower-caste Hindus, because he came to believe that everyone has equal status in the eyes of God. Sikhs rejected the caste system, and called for closer ties between Hindus and Muslims.

Nanak wrote his religious teachings in Punjabi, the language normally spoken in northern India, rather than in Sanskrit, the learned language in which most formal Hindu texts were written. Like the Protestant reformers who were preaching in Germany at the same time, Nanak thought it was important that people who were not members of the educated elite have access to religious writings. Sikhs shared certain aspects of belief with the followers of other religions in India: like Hindus, they believed in reincarnation; like Muslims, they rejected the use of religious images; and like Parsis, they taught that believers

A marble statue of a Jain saint sits in a position for meditation. The founder of Jainism, Mahavira, urged his followers to meditate, live simply, and never kill another living thing.

The Truest and Mightiest Religion

MUHAMMAD AKBAR, SPEECH DELIVERED TO THE SCHOLARS OF MANY RELIGIONS AT HIS COURT, 1580

A group of Portuguese Jesuit priests came to Akbar's court in 1580 and stayed for several years, participating in the religious discussions he supported. The Jesuits were clearly impressed with Akbar, describing him in letters from the early 1580s as "a great patron of learning" with "excellent judgment and a good memory." They also commented on how effective he was at collecting taxes and supporting trade, both of which provided "enormous sums" for the royal treasury. In this speech, written down by Father Monserrate, one of the Jesuit priests, Akbar discusses his religious interests.

I perceive that there are varying customs and beliefs of varying religious paths. For the teachings of the Hindus, the Muslims, the Parsis, the Jews, and the Christians are all different. But the followers of each religion regard the institutions of their own religion as better than those of any other. Not only so, but they strive to convert the rest to their own way of belief. If these refuse to be converted, they not only despise them, but also regard them for this very reason as their enemies. And this causes me to feel many serious doubts and scruples. Wherefore I desire that on appointed days the books of all religious laws be brought forward, and the doctors [of the study of religion] meet and hold discussions, so that I may hear them, and that each one may determine which is the truest and mightiest religion.

The Mughal sultan Akbar receives visitors at his court. As any ruler would expect, these visiting noblemen bring gifts, including a deer and other animals, to show their esteem.

should actively resist evil rather than concentrate only on the next life. Some people see Sikhism as a blend of other religions, or a reformed version of Hinduism, but most Sikhs see it as a new religion, with its most important ideas coming directly from God through Nanak's revelations.

Akbar gathered Muslims, Hindus, Parsis, Sikhs, Christians, and scholars of other faiths together for discussions. "Crowds of learned men from all nations, and sages of various religions," wrote a Muslim historian in a letter in 1580, "came to the Court and were honored." In 1582 he went further, establishing what he called the Divine Faith, which combined ideas and rituals from many religions. The Divine Faith also included ceremonies showing respect for Akbar—Akbar clearly saw himself as the center of this new religion. Loyalty to the emperor, he thought, along with shared religious ideas, would unite India's many religious and ethnic groups. Most of his courtiers supported him in this new religion, capturing its spirit in the phrase "Allahu Akbar," which, because of the meaning of Akbar, means both "God is greater than anything else" and "God is Akbar." More traditional Muslim scholars were horrified at this phrase, seeing it as emperor worship, which is strictly forbidden in Islam.

Guru Nanak founded the Sikh religion in the early 1500s. Sikhism spread from Nanak's homeland in northern India, and today is ranked as the world's fifth-largest religion.

This new Divine Faith did not last much beyond Akbar's death. Fifty years after his death, his bones were dug up and thrown away by an angry mob. (Similarly, Protestants in Europe dug up the bones of saints, to show that they were not to be honored.) Hostilities between Hindus, Muslims, and Sikhs shaped the history of south Asia from then on. Like Akbar, the 20th-century Indian leader Mohandas Gandhi hoped to create a state where the followers of different religions would live in peace. Gandhi was assassinated in 1947 by a Hindu fanatic, and religious disputes continue to lead to violence in South Asia today.

The musicians of that territory breathed fascination with the instruments of their country, especially with the organ. Ear and eye were delighted and so was the mind.

—Akbar's chief advisor, in a history of the court called the *Akbarnama,* describing Portuguese musicians visiting Akbar's court in the 1590s

Although Akbar's religion died out quickly, he set a pattern for communication between cultures that extended beyond religion and did last longer. Painters at the Mughal court combined Persian technical skills and Indian ideas about the importance of nature in book illustrations and portraits, and later added ways of showing perspective that came from Renaissance Europe. The magnificent Mughal style can be seen in the Taj Mahal.

Akbar's grandson Shah Jahan built this mosque and tomb in the middle of the 17th century for his beloved wife Mumtaz (a word that means "excellent") Mahal. The Taj Mahal took 20,000 workers almost 20 years to build, and is considered by many people to be the most beautiful building in the world. Like the visitors to the Süleymaniye in Istanbul, those who see the Taj Mahal often can "not find terms to express their astonishment."

The Taj Mahal was built as a mosque and tomb for the adored wife of Mughal sultan Shah Jahan. He was later imprisoned by his son, and spent his last years in a tiny cell where he could see the Taj Mahal only in a reflection in a mirror.

CHAPTER 7

GUTS, GAIN, AND GLORY

POWERFUL MONARCHS IN ENGLAND AND AFRICA

Try to imagine yourself in this story: Your father was a king, and his first wife was a princess, but she did not give birth to a son but only to one somewhat sickly daughter. Your father decided to divorce her in order to marry your mother, hoping she would give him a son to inherit the kingdom, even though earlier he had had an affair with your mother's sister. But the pope would not allow him to divorce, because the pope was being held prisoner by your mother's nephew. So your father dropped his allegiance to the pope, taking his kingdom with him, and set up his own church that let him get divorced.

This portrait of Elizabeth Tudor was painted when she was 14, at the request of her younger brother Edward, who had just become king. When she sent it to him, she wrote, "when you look on my picture . . . think that as you have the outward shadow of my body before you, so my inward mind wisheth that the body itself were oftener in your presence."

His hopes for a son were dashed when you (a girl) were born, so when you were two he invented charges of adultery against your mother, declared that she had bewitched him, and had her and her brother executed. Meanwhile you were sent away, and shuffled from one country house to another. Your father married a third time, and this wife did have a son, but died in childbirth. He married a fourth time to a foreigner he had never seen, but as soon as the two met they hated each other and the marriage ended. He married a fifth time, to a much younger woman, who had an affair, so he had her executed as well, when you were eight. He married a sixth time, to a widow about his age who liked you and invited you back into the household.

When you are fourteen, your father dies and your younger half-brother, who is nine, becomes king. He dies six years later of tuberculosis, having named your 16-year-old cousin as queen. But your older half-sister thinks she should be queen, and the law and most of the people agree, so after nine days your cousin and her husband are arrested and thrown in prison. Your half-sister becomes queen, and executes people who disagree with her about religion. She also decides to marry the king of a foreign country. This sets off a rebellion. Your half-sister thinks your cousin is involved with the rebellion, so she beheads her and her husband. Your half-sister thinks that you're involved, too, so she has you arrested and sent to the same prison where your mother, your stepmother, and your cousin were executed. "I most humbly beseech your majesty," you write to her, "to remember your last promise, that I be not condemned without answer and due proof." No proof is found, so after two

King Henry VIII of England plays a small harp as his court fool stands to the side. Court entertainments included music, plays, jousts, trained animals, dancing, juggling, and comedy routines, and rulers often participated in the festivities.

months you are released, and then you try to stay as far away from your half-sister as you can. All this happens before your 21st birthday.

If you proposed this story as the plot of a soap opera, television executives would probably say that it was not believable, and perhaps too full of sex and violence to be shown to children. It's not fiction, however, but the real girlhood of Elizabeth Tudor, who became Queen Elizabeth I of England in 1555, four years after she got out of prison. Elizabeth's father was Henry VIII, who first married Catherine of Aragon, the daughter of Ferdinand and Isabella, the rulers of Spain. Catherine's daughter was Mary, and her nephew was Charles V, the emperor of Germany, whose troops were in Rome at the time Henry wanted his (first) divorce. When the pope refused to grant the divorce, Henry declared that England was no longer part of the Catholic Church, and set up a separate church, in which he would appoint the highest official. (This official, the archbishop of Canterbury, issued Henry's divorce.)

Elizabeth's mother was Anne Boleyn, an English noblewoman and lady-in-waiting at the court, whose sister Mary had been one of Henry's mistresses. Henry's third wife was Jane Seymour, who gave birth to Edward, who became Edward VI. (Kings and queens don't get numbers after their names until they actually become rulers.) His hated fourth wife was Anne of Cleves, a German princess; his unfaithful fifth wife was Catherine Howard, an English noblewoman; and his sixth wife, the widow, was Katherine Parr, also an English noblewoman. Elizabeth's ill-fated cousin was Lady Jane Grey, who was imprisoned and beheaded in the Tower of London, where Elizabeth was imprisoned as well.

Elizabeth's half-sister Mary, like her mother Isabella, was a firm Catholic, and during her reign she had about 300 Protestants arrested and executed. Mary married the Catholic King Philip II of Spain, who later sent the Spanish Armada against Elizabeth. During Mary's reign, some prominent Protestants fled to France, Germany, and Switzerland, and, after her death of natural causes, gave her the nickname "Bloody Mary."

No crooked leg, no bleared eye,
No part deformed out of kind,
Nor yet so ugly half can be
As is the inward suspicious mind.

—Queen Elizabeth I, poem handwritten in her French prayer book, about 1555

FROM THE TOWER OF LONDON TO THE TOP OF THE WORLD

We would certainly understand if a person with this violent family history was deeply troubled and never amounted to much, but Elizabeth instead became one of the most effective monarchs England (or any country) ever had. While moving around, she gained a good education, so she could read, write, and speak several languages. Later, in negotiations with a group of Polish ambassadors, she argued with them so effectively in Latin (the only language they had in common) that she got everything she wanted. In foreign affairs, she followed the example of her grandfather, Henry VII, who had also used diplomacy instead of armies to get what England needed. Like her grandfather—but not her father, who had nearly bankrupted England—Elizabeth was thrifty and shrewd, supporting foreign trade and the domestic manufacture of woolen cloth because they brought in taxes.

At a time when most rulers and almost all people with political power were men, you might think that being a woman would be a disadvantage, but Elizabeth turned this into an asset. When she inherited the throne at 25, she was the most eligible unmarried woman in all of Europe. Foreign princes, including Philip II (her half-sister Mary's former husband), and English nobles all hoped they might be the lucky choice. They sent letters, dispatched ambassadors, and came to her court themselves. At her court, Elizabeth entertained them politely and lavishly, holding banquets, parties, sailing races, concerts, and theater performances.

She encouraged first one suitor and then another, using the possibility of marrying her as a tool of foreign policy and a way to gain the allegiance of

Elizabeth is carried in a royal procession by her armed guards, and accompanied by courtiers and court ladies. Elizabeth understood that personal appearances increased the loyalty of her subjects, some of whom can be seen lining the streets and crowding balconies to get a glimpse of her.

The Heart and Stomach of a King

ELIZABETH I, SPEECH BEFORE ENGLISH TROOPS, TILBURY, ENGLAND, 1588

Right after the defeat of the Spanish Armada, Queen Elizabeth went to Tilbury, in southern England, where her troops were gathered. There are reports that she wore a fancy armor breastplate—Elizabeth had an excellent sense of style and gave a stirring speech to a large crowd. She praised the bravery of her soldiers, and persuaded her people that she could be a strong ruler even though she was not a man. She uses the word "stomach" to mean the same thing that we do when we say "guts"—courage that comes from inside.

My loving people: we [rulers often use the plural to speak about themselves] have been persuaded by some that are careful of our safety to take heed how we commit ourselves to armed multitudes for fear of treachery. But I assure you I do not desire to live to distrust my faithful and loving people. Let tyrants fear. I have always so behaved myself that, under God, I have placed my chiefest strength and safeguard in the loyal hearts and goodwill of my subjects. And therefore I am come amongst you, as you see, at this time, not for my recreation and disport [showing off], but being resolved in the midst and heat of the battle to live or die amongst you all, to lay down for my God, and for my kingdom, and for my people, my honor and my blood, even in the dust. I know I have the body of a weak and feeble woman, but I have the heart and stomach of a king—and of a king of England, too. I think foul scorn that Parma [a leader of the Spanish Armada], or Spain, or any prince of Europe should dare to invade the borders of my realm. To which, rather than any dishonor shall grow by men, I myself will take up arms. I myself will be your general, judge, and rewarder.

Elizabeth's beautiful signature appeared on a royal proclamation. The "R" after her name stands for Regina, the Latin word for queen. British coins today have a picture of the second Queen Elizabeth, and the letters ER.

different groups within England. She was a Protestant, but when she didn't marry a Protestant, her Catholic subjects, with only a few exceptions, remained loyal. Her advisors and other political leaders in England wanted desperately for her to marry so that there would be an heir to the throne, but she told them bluntly in a speech that it was her decision to make and not theirs, "whose duties are to obey." She never explained to anyone exactly why she didn't marry, though she hinted that it was because she knew that if she did, she would have to share power with her husband. From her own childhood, she certainly had enough experience with the problems that marriage could bring.

Elizabeth had also seen the problems that religious disagreements could bring. Both her father and sister had executed people for their religious beliefs, and religious wars had been going on in some part of Europe since the day she was born. Elizabeth knew that one of the first things she would have to do after she became queen was decide whether England's religion would be Catholic or Protestant, and to carry out her decision without causing a revolt.

Elizabeth's father had set up the Church of England, which was Protestant in most of its doctrines and rituals. Services were in English, priests were allowed to marry, and monasteries were closed. Elizabeth's half-sister Mary had tried to abolish this church and make England Catholic again, which some people supported and others opposed. Elizabeth reestablished a non-Catholic Church of England, but she realized that people in England varied widely in their interpretations of Christian teachings. Like the Mughal emperor Akbar, she sought to bring religious peace by allowing a certain level of religious diversity. As long as people were loyal to her, she did not want to "make windows into men's souls," that is, know exactly what they believed.

Elizabeth also stayed out of foreign wars as long as she could, which helped keep the royal treasury full. When the Spanish Armada threatened to invade England in 1588, she was drawn into international conflict, but the benefits of her religious policy became clear. Catholics in England supported their queen, not the Catholic king of Spain.

This spinet, a keyboard instrument that was an early version of the piano, is decorated with the royal coat of arms and may have belonged to Queen Elizabeth. Like her father, Elizabeth enjoyed music and dancing, so composers and musicians flocked to her court.

Elizabeth ruled for 45 years, one of the longest reigns in English history. During this time, often called the "Elizabethan Age," literature and the arts flourished. Shakespeare and other playwrights wrote and put on their plays. Composers and musicians developed new styles in music, including music for dancing, which Elizabeth loved to do. Many writers hoped to gain royal favor—and financial support—so they wrote poems, music, and essays in Elizabeth's honor, praising her as "Gloriana." English explorers paid tribute to her by naming the part of North America they claimed for England "Virginia," in honor of her status as a virgin queen. Despite the problems she encountered toward the end of her reign, most people agreed with Elizabeth's description of herself in her last speech to government officials in 1601: "There will never Queen sit in my seat with more zeal to my country, care for my subjects, and that will sooner with willingness venture her life for your good and safety, than me."

In many ways Elizabeth was unique. No other woman anywhere in the world during her lifetime had as much power as she did, and very few rulers used their power as wisely. In other ways, however, the problems she faced were similar to those faced by kings and queens all over the world: How could they keep the land that they ruled strong? How could they keep it prosperous? How should they handle religious differences among their subjects? We have already seen some of the ways in which Suleyman the Magnificent, Ferdinand and Isabella, Akbar, and Elizabeth dealt with such problems. What about rulers in other parts of the world?

TIMBUKTU AND THE KONGO, TOO

Sunni Ali Ber, the ruler of a small area in western Africa, conquered his neighbors in the late 15th century and built an empire called the Songhay Empire around three important cities on the Niger River, Gao, Jenne, and Timbuktu. He appointed officials to oversee his territory and set up a navy to patrol the Niger River. He increased the size of the army, and provided more training for its soldiers. Like the Italian cities of Florence and Venice, the Songhay cities grew wealthy through trade. Traders brought salt, textiles, and metal goods across the Sahara Desert by camel, and exchanged them for gold and slaves that came up the Niger River by ship and canoe.

The Great Mosque at Timbuktu, the oldest mosque south of the Sahara Desert, was built during the 14th century. This building combines features distinctive to Islam, such as the tower at the top from which a chanter calls people to prayer, with features common to buildings in this part of the world, such as its squarish shape and brick construction.

Timbuktu (in the present-day West African country of Mali) was an important center of Islamic scholarship and book production. It attracted many visitors, including Leo Africanus, a Muslim scholar who had been expelled from Spain as a young boy, captured by pirates, given as a slave to the pope, and sent by the pope in 1526 to conduct a survey of Africa. He wrote that, "more profit is made from the trade in books than from any other line of business." The city was home to three universities and many schools that taught the Quran (the holy book of Islam). Though Sunni Ali Ber was officially a Muslim, he thought that the scholars of Timbuktu, some of whom were Arabs from North Africa and the Middle East, did not pay enough respect to the African religions that people had followed before Islam came to West Africa. Traditional African religions often focused on making offerings, saying specific phrases, or doing rituals to encourage good spirits to help believers and bad spirits to leave them alone.

These actions were similar to those that European Christians were doing at the same time, when they asked saints for assistance and prayed that demons stay away. Sunni Ali threatened to arrest the Timbuktu scholars, and many of them fled the city.

The scholars returned when one of Sunni Ali's generals, who had different ideas about religion, took over the throne at the end of the 15th century. This new monarch, Askia (which means "king" in the Songhay languages) Muhammad Turé became known as Askia the Great. He thought that Islam would be more helpful in making the Songhay Empire strong and unified than traditional religions, so he used Islamic scholars as advisors on legal and political matters, supported the building of mosques, and encouraged the writing of books on Muslim history and law.

Askia the Great paid attention to things other than religion as well. He divided the empire into well-governed provinces and appointed honest officials. Like Henry VII in England, who was ruling at the same time, he encouraged trade as a way to increase the amount of money coming in to the royal treasury. The Songhay Empire continued to expand its borders under Askia the Great, becoming the largest and wealthiest kingdom ever in this part of Africa.

The western African artist who carved this ivory spoon in the 16th century may have used a Portuguese spoon as a model, but he included a figure carved according to local traditions.

South of the Songhay Empire, rulers in the Kingdom of Kongo also built a powerful state that included parts of what are now the Republic of Congo, Zaire, and Angola. A manikongo, or king, who had both political and religious power ruled Kongo, appointing governors and other officials who oversaw the collection of taxes and recruitment of soldiers. People followed traditional African religions, and saw the rituals and offerings of the manikongo as especially strong and effective in influencing the world of the spirits.

Islam never spread to the Kingdom of Kongo, but at the end of the 15th century Portuguese Catholic missionaries introduced Christianity. The missionaries soon gained converts, including the manikongo, who raised his children as Christians. When his son Nzinga Mbemba, who took the Christian name Afonso I, came to power, he worked to convert his subjects to Christianity. Many Christian ideas were

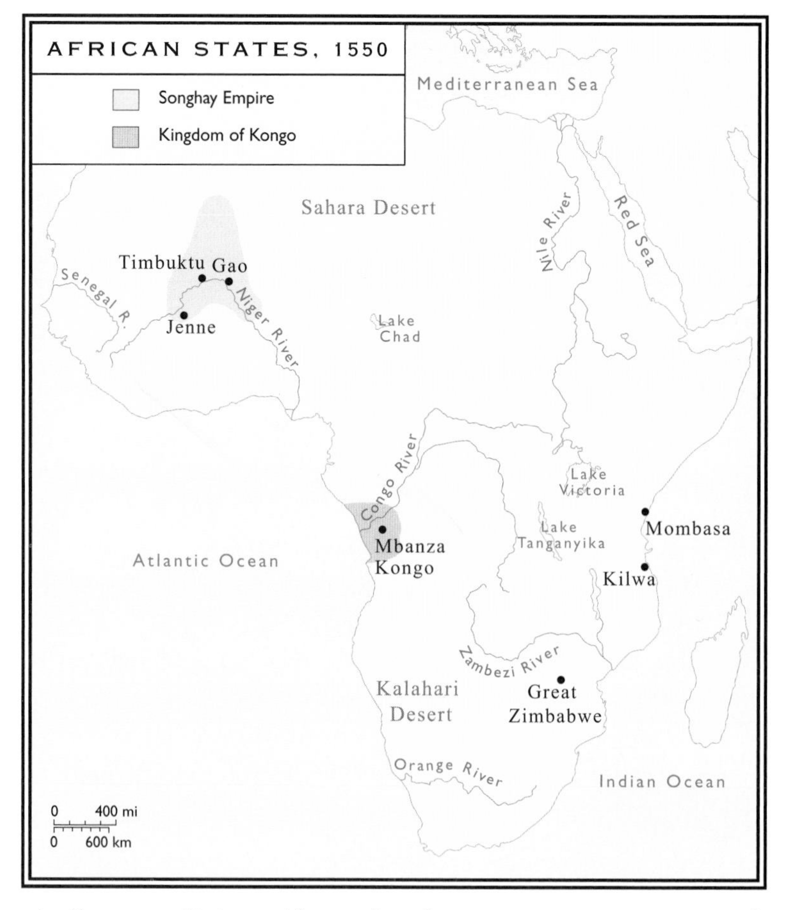

similar to religious ideas already present in Kongo. Both Christianity and traditional African religions taught that there was a heaven, that angels and demons helped and hurt people, and that priests had special powers. Both had an initiation ritual involving water that signified rebirth. These similarities meant it was not difficult for many people to accept Christian teachings, especially with their ruler's encouragement. Afonso I built so many churches in the Kongolese capital city, Mbanza, that people called it "Kongo of the Bell."

Missionaries were not the only people who came from Portugal to Kongo, however. Merchants—who brought cloth, horses, and weapons, and traded them for gold, silver, ivory, and slaves—and advisors came in much greater numbers than the missionaries. At first, their dealings with the Portuguese increased the power and wealth of the kings of Kongo. Soon, however, the trade in slaves weakened the kingdom. The Portuguese sometimes raided villages and captured slaves on their own, but more often they worked with local leaders, who provided them with slaves in exchange for guns and other merchandise. These leaders started wars so that they would have captives to sell as slaves, or just grabbed people from their houses and fields. Slave traders, both Portuguese and African, from coastal areas went farther and farther inland to capture, buy, or trade for more and more slaves.

"Merchants take every day our natives," wrote Afonso I in a letter to the king of Portugal in 1526, "grab them, and get them to be sold." "Our country is being completely depopulated," he reported, "and your Highness should not agree with this nor accept it as in your service." The slave trade was encouraging wars and destroying families, and he pleaded, "We beg of your Highness to help and assist us, because it is our will that in these kingdoms there should not be any trade of slaves." He suggested that instead the king send "two physicians" with "good drugs and medi-

Many of our people, desirous of the wares of your Kingdoms... seize [others] of our people... and take them to be sold.... And as soon as they are taken by the white men they are immediately branded with fire.

—King Afonso I of Kongo, letter to King John III of Portugal, 1526

King Dom Garcia II of the Kongo greets Catholic missionaries in 1648. This drawing was made by one of the missionaries, who lived in the Kongo more than a century after Christianity was first introduced there.

"There are many judges, doctors, and clerics here, all receiving good salaries from King Askia Mohamed of the State of Songhay. He pays great respect to men of learning. There is a great demand for books."

—16th-century historian Leo Africanus on Timbuktu, "Description of Africa," 1526

cine" to help against "many and different diseases." These diseases were killing "many of those who had already been instructed in the holy faith of Our Lord Jesus Christ," so that people were turning away from Christianity and trying "herbs and ceremonies and other ancient methods" as cures. Despite these pleas, the king of Portugal did nothing, and the slave trade flourished. In fact, one in five African Americans is descended from people who were originally from Kongo. The slave trade weakened the authority of the manikongo, and the Kingdom of Kongo slowly broke apart.

What do Elizabeth, Askia the Great, and Afonso I have in common? All three of them used well-equipped armies, efficient tax collectors, and capable officials to build up their own power and the power of the territories they ruled. They encouraged trade and commerce, and taxed this trade so that more money came into their treasuries. They recognized that religion was important to their people, and helped certain religions to become stronger. We know almost nothing about the early life of Askia the Great, and only a little more about that of Afonso I, so we cannot tell how their boyhoods affected them. We can say that for at least one 16th-century ruler, a truly chaotic and turbulent childhood did not keep her from being determined and effective. Elizabeth set her country on a path that would eventually lead it to create an empire that spread all over the world. English people did not create this empire alone, however, but also with the labor of native peoples and African slaves.

CHAPTER 8

"EVERYTHING THE WORLD HAS TO OFFER"

CITY LIFE

Soon after his 18th birthday, a wealthy eastern European nobleman, Baron Waldstein, left the small German city of Strasbourg on the Rhine River, where he was a university student, for a grand tour of the major cities of Europe. He went to Paris, Geneva (Switzerland), and Amsterdam (Holland), and in the summer of 1600, to London, keeping a diary of his travels. What did he see and do in London? Like many travelers, he "spent time in lively and interesting conversation," and also watched "a group of thieves and robbers on their way to be hanged." He walked along the Thames River, which flows through the city and was "so thick on all sides with the masts and sails of vessels that one might imagine it a closely entwined forest." "This placid river," he writes, "is a centre of trade for everything the world has to offer."

The Tower of London, with boats on the River Thames in the foreground and London Bridge—which spanned the Thames—in the background. Leaning out of a window is one of the Tower's many important prisoners, a French nobleman who had been captured by the English during the Hundred Years' War.

He and his companions "went to see an English play," in a theater "built of wood and so designed that the spectators can get a comfortable view of everything that happens in any part of the building." This could have been the Globe Theatre, where Shakespeare put on many of his plays, but Baron Waldstein doesn't tell us, nor does he tell us what play he saw. He does give a very long description of visiting the royal chapels in Westminster Abbey, with their "splendid tombs" and "magnificent workmanship." He toured Whitehall Palace, with its royal portraits and gardens, where he saw a "rib bone from a most enormous whale which is well worth seeing."

Just like visitors to London still do, he toured the Tower of London, which housed a

Acrobats perform an act with a goose on an Italian city street. Afterward they would pass a hat for money, and the people watching them would be easy targets for pickpockets.

collection of animals, including "three great lions and two lionesses, a leopard, a tiger, and a huge porcupine," as well as a "fine collection of cannon, pikes [heavy spears], shields, arrows, cross-bows, javelins and other weapons." The baron was especially impressed with "iron devices which they fire from naval guns to destroy ships' rigging," and "barbed arrows which at the same time pierce the flesh and burn from the pitch smeared on them." He saw the room where Queen Elizabeth had been held prisoner, and a courtyard with four scaffolds where several nobles had been executed for treason.

The Tower was not the only place where Baron Waldstein was confronted with the consequences of disloyalty. Shortly before his visit, there had been a rebellion against Queen Elizabeth, and attached to a bridge were poles with "the heads of earls and other noblemen who have been executed for treason." One afternoon he "went to see the bears," public spectacles called bearbaitings held twice a week in which hungry dogs were set upon a chained bear to see which animal would tear the other apart. Afterward he went to the house of an acquaintance, where he "saw six girls—all sisters and of a good family—who sang and played most beautifully on various kinds of musical instruments." His visit ended with an audience with Queen Elizabeth and a "very grand dinner by the Mayor of London."

The inhabitants of this city are engaged in commerce and are very rich... they are courteous, civil, ingenious, quick to imitate foreigners, and to intermarry with them. In all possible ways appear the wealth, power, pomp, and magnificence of this city.

—Italian merchant and author Ludovico Guicciardini, describing the northern European city of Antwerp in a survey of cities for Italian travelers, 1560

MY CITY IS GREATER THAN YOUR CITY

Baron Waldstein was a wealthy noble, so he saw and did things on his trip to London that more ordinary visitors to the city would not, but he was also a typical young traveler, reporting enthusiastically about all the city offered. Travelers to other cities in the 15th and 16th centuries also kept diaries and wrote letters about what they had seen. From these and other kinds of historical documents, we can discover what city life was like. Most of the people in the world lived in small villages and made their living by raising crops, but towns and cities offered opportunities that could lead to a better, or at least a different, life. By the time Baron Waldstein visited London, some cities had grown huge, with hundreds of thousands of residents. China had more large cities than any other part of the world, but many of the things that Baron Waldstein saw in London would greet a visitor in almost any large city.

Visitors to any city would find shopkeepers and public markets selling imported luxuries and locally produced goods. The world's first "shopping mall" was built in London in 1568. It was an enclosed market with shops on the ground floor and upper gallery, a setup found in many malls today. Many cities were built on rivers or along seacoasts, and their harbors brought in merchandise from all over the world, though even those that were not on water offered exotic goods from far away. In southern Africa, merchants in the city of Great Zimbabwe sold cloth and beads from India and Indonesia, and even porcelain from China, all of which came across the Indian Ocean. Like the goods in their markets, city people came from many places. In Istanbul, the capital of the Ottoman Empire, people of all sorts lived and did business in its crowded, narrow streets: Greeks, Serbs, Albanians, Venetians (from Venice), Turks, Armenians, Bulgarians, and Genoese (from the northern Italian city of Genoa).

Customers and shopkeepers bargain in a narrow Italian city street specifically set up for fabric and furniture merchants. In the foreground are stalls selling cloth and clothing, and in the background are stalls with wooden benches and chests.

"Our beautiful Florence contains within the city 277 shops of wool merchants," wrote a proud citizen of Florence in 1472 in a letter to a friend in Venice, "and eighty-three rich and splendid warehouses of silk-merchants." His city also produced goods, with 84 shops of cabinetmakers, 54 stonecutters, 44 goldsmiths, 30 jewelers, 66 grocers, 70 butchers, and "artists in wax" making candles and wax figures better than those in "all the cities of the world." But Venice was just as wealthy, wrote a German visitor a few years after the man from Florence had bragged to his friend in Venice, with "stores full of merchandise, spices, rare cloths, silk draperies and many other goods."

Many of the world's largest cities were capitals, filled with officials, nobles, lawyers, and bureaucrats all hoping to gain power and influence through their dealings with the ruler. London was a capital, and so were Istanbul, Paris, and Rome.

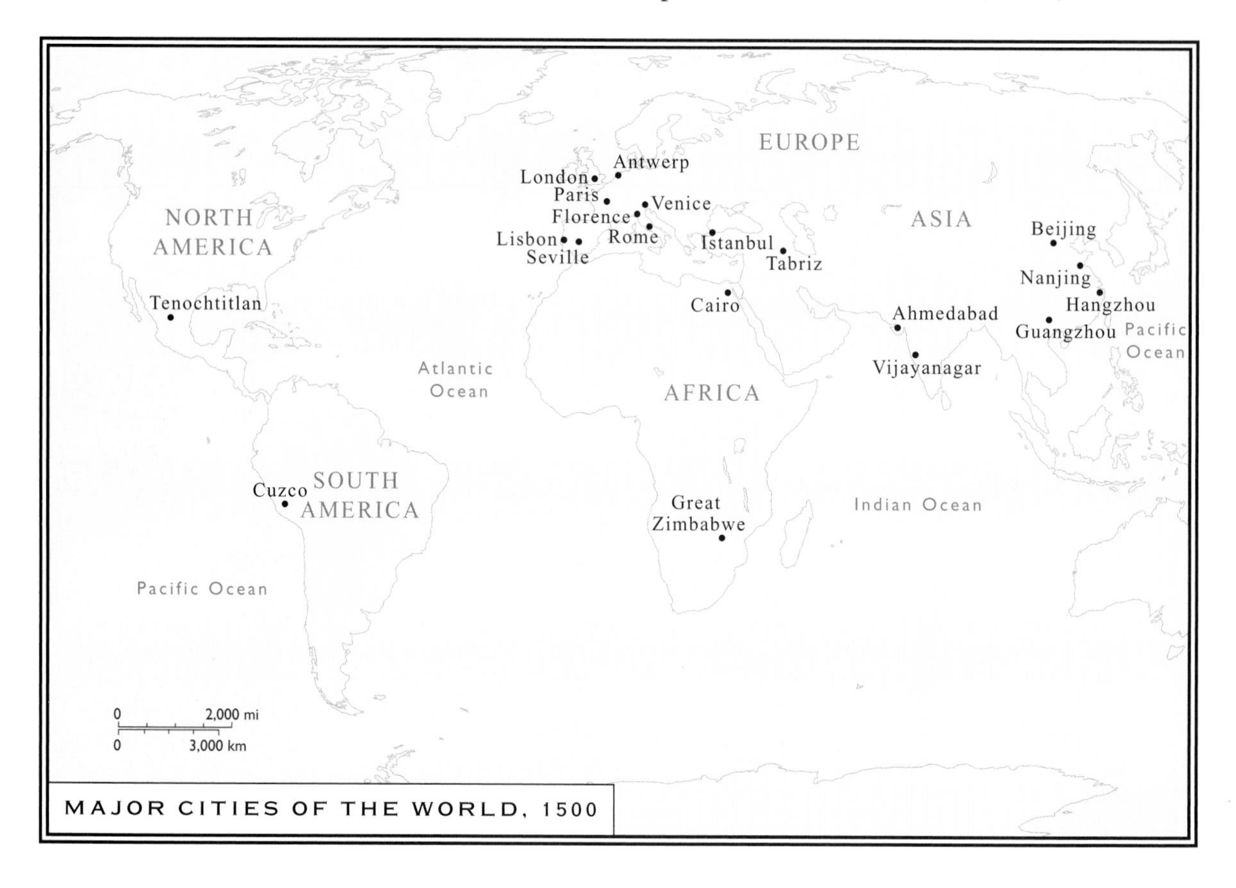

MAJOR CITIES OF THE WORLD, 1500

The pope was the ruler of the city of Rome and much of the surrounding countryside, as well as being the head of the Catholic Church. Bishops, lawyers, and officials hoping to advance in the church hierarchy all came to Rome, where the popes were spending vast amounts of money building and decorating churches and palaces. The Sistine Chapel, where Michelangelo and Pope Julius II argued so often, was part of the expanded and improved papal palace called the Vatican, built over several centuries.

The streets of Osaka, one of the largest cities in 17th-century Japan, were crowded during the day with shoppers, businessmen, and all sorts of people. At night, cloth screens advertising things to buy were unrolled down over the front of the stalls.

In China, Beijing (which means "northern capital) was the largest city. Originally named Khanbalik, it had been the capital of the Mongol Empire under Khublai Khan. The Ming emperors made it their capital as well, and had palaces and temples built in many different architectural styles. The largest of these, and, in fact, the world's largest palace complex, was the Forbidden City, with almost 10,000 buildings. Only those on imperial business were officially allowed to enter—this is why it was "forbidden"—but this included tens of thousands of servants, cooks, laborers, and messengers, so there were many common people in the palace every day. The walls of the Forbidden City are thick and squat, and were specifically designed to withstand cannon attacks. There were also larger rings of walls circling much of the city, and another set of walls surrounding some of the suburbs. These multiple sets of walls still did not surround all the people who streamed into Beijing, which had about 600,000 residents by 1600. Even though Confucian tradition considered trade the lowest occupation, and scholarship the highest, many Beijing merchants in Ming China became wealthy.

There is great wealth of all sorts in this city, some in the royal palaces and some in the houses of the mighty, some in the homes of the common people, and still other, finer and more abundant, laid up in the churches.

—Ottoman ruler Mehmed I describing Constantinople right before he conquered it in 1453, from a history written by one of his officials

In India, Ahmedabad in the Gujarat province of northwestern India was probably the largest city, with about 200,000 residents in 1600. In the 15th century, Ahmed Shah,

The palace complex, or Forbidden City, occupies a huge area in the center of Beijing. Like many buildings in China, the Forbidden City was laid out according to principles of feng shui, *the ancient Chinese art of arranging things to create a harmonious and healthy environment.*

the ruler of this part of India, founded the city and made it his capital, expanding and reinforcing its walls. He filled the city with beautiful mosques and gardens. Weavers in Ahmedabad specialized in making fine cotton cloth, which was exported as far as Europe and China.

In the Americas, the largest city was Tenochtitlan, built by the Aztecs in the 14th century on the shores and islands of Lake Texcoco in central Mexico. The Aztecs chose this site because it fit with a religious prophecy, and at first it was not a very easy to place to live. They dredged earth from the bottom of the lake to make the islands larger, and also to build floating fields of heaped-up mud and plants, called *chinampas,* for growing crops. They built causeways connecting the islands to the shore, and a huge religious center with many temples and courtyards. By 1500, several hundred thousand people lived in and around the city of Tenochtitlan.

THIS CITY STINKS!

Cities were places of leisure as well as work. Baron Waldstein went to plays and bearbaitings, and if he had wanted, he could have attended the hanging of the thieves and robbers he watched being led away, because executions were public events. People gathered in large crowds to watch especially notorious criminals be hanged or beheaded, and the bodies and the heads were displayed for days, weeks, or even months afterward. Small villages often did not have scaffolds or other places of execution, and most law courts were in towns and cities, so people came from far and wide for trials and punishments.

Some types of activities attracted everyone, but others were more often shared with people of the same sex and age. Adult men in cities often gathered in public places such

Good Houses and Pleasant Gardens

HERNÁN CORTÉS, LETTER TO KING CHARLES I OF SPAIN, 1520

Hernán Cortés was the Spanish military leader who conquered the Aztec Empire in 1521. In this letter to his king, he compares the Aztec city Tenochtitlan to various Spanish cities that he has visited.

This great city of Tenochtitlan is built on the salt lake, and no matter by what road you travel there are two leagues [about 7 miles] from the main body of the city to the mainland. There are four artificial causeways leading to it, and each is as wide as two cavalry lances. The city itself is as big as Seville or Córdoba. The main streets are very wide and very straight; some of these are on the land, but the rest and all the smaller ones are half on land, half canals where they paddle their canoes.

This city has many squares where trading is done and markets are held continuously. There is also one square twice as big as that of Salamanca, with arcades all around, where more than sixty thousand people come each day to buy and sell, and where every kind of merchandise produced in these lands is found: provisions as well as ornaments of gold and silver, lead, brass, copper, tin, stones, shells, bones, and feathers. . . . There is in this great square a very large building like a courthouse, where ten or twelve persons sit as judges. They preside over all that happens in the markets, and sentence criminals.

There are, in all districts of this great city, many temples. . . .There are in the city many large and beautiful houses, and the reason for this is that all the chiefs in the lands, who are Moctezuma's vassals [men who owe allegiance to Moctezuma], have houses in the city and live there for part of the year; and in addition there are many rich citizens who likewise have very good houses. All of these houses have very large and very good rooms and also very pleasant gardens of various sorts of flowers both on the upper and lower floors.

A modern Mexican artist's idea of what Tenochtitlan looked like when it was the Aztec capital. Causeways link the island city with the shore, and floating islands provide places to plant beans, squash, and other crops.

as town squares, mosques, tearooms and coffeehouses, or taverns, where they discussed the day's events, worshipped together, and often shared food and beverages. Adult women in many parts of the world were more secluded, socializing in their homes rather than in public. The adult women who did appear regularly in public were often in occupations regarded as dishonorable for a woman, such as musicians, actresses, and waitresses in taverns. Women in London did spend some time in public, though the girls Waldstein watched playing instruments were in their own home, not on a public stage. Whatever play he attended certainly did not feature female actors, for in Shakespeare's London men played all the parts.

Along with work and leisure, worship was also an important activity in cities. Baron Waldstein visited St. Paul's and other churches in London, and visitors to Rome, Istanbul, Ahmedabad, and Tenochtitlan all commented on the cities' religious buildings. Some of these buildings were crowded with worshippers, altars, and artwork, while others were more serene places, where people could go to escape the bustle of the city's streets.

Those busy streets made cities exciting, but they also made them unhealthy. Bubonic plague, tuberculosis, typhoid, and smallpox spread easily in crowded conditions, so in cities there were far more deaths than births. The cities grew because immigrants poured into the cities from the countryside, making the city still more crowded as spaces between buildings were filled with new housing. Fire was a constant danger. The Great Fire of London in 1666 destroyed more than 13,000 homes and nearly 100 churches, including the St. Paul's that Baron Waldstein visited. (A new and larger St. Paul's was built in its place.) Crime was another problem, and the thieves and robbers Baron Waldstein saw being taken off for execution would not have been an unusual sight.

Beggars would have also been a common sight. Especially during times of famine or war, cities became filled with beggars and people seeking support from churches or other charitable groups. Cities sometimes rounded up beggars and other poor people, banishing them beyond the city walls and punishing them physically with whipping, branding, or cutting off their earlobes if they returned. (Being "branded a thief" was a real punishment, not just an expression.) Men might be sent into forced military service, especially rowing galleys and other types of ships that fought in naval battles.

Children who were caught begging might be sold into slavery, or, in European cities, transported to the new colonies as indentured servants, required to work without

People who had lost limbs to leprosy and soldiers who had been injured in war joined other beggars on city streets. Beggars with contagious illnesses were often required to make noise to warn people that they were coming. One of these beggars has bands of bells around his legs for that purpose.

This typical French city woman from the 16th century might have been the wife of the glassmaker who crafted this tiny part of a huge stained-glass cathedral window. To anyone seeing it from the floor, this figure would have looked simply like a bit of golden glass—only the artist (and God, of course) knew she was there.

pay for a certain period of time for the person who paid for their passage. In 1620, the city council of London arranged for "one hundred children out of their superfluous multitude [the great number of beggar children] to be transported to Virginia, there to be bound apprentices." The councilmen picked these children off the streets or from orphanages, but some of the children "declared their unwillingness to go." The city did not have the authority to send "these persons against their wills," so officials of the company organizing the Virginia colony asked the royal council for permission. The city council was especially eager to have these "ill disposed and impudent" children sent away, so that "in Virginia under severe masters they may be brought to goodness." Permission was granted, and the children were taken to Virginia.

Baron Waldstein does not mention poor children or beggars in his diary, probably because he didn't notice much about them. There are other things he also doesn't comment on because they were so familiar, but that we would find very striking if we were suddenly transported back to a 16th-century city. Nights would be dark, with streets that were fairly quiet. Artificial light came from candles and torches, so people worked when there was sunlight. Many cities had curfews restricting movement after dark, figuring that only those up to no good were out at night. Night watchmen patrolled the streets, watching for crime and fire.

The people who worked, as opposed to the very rich and the very poor, were not gathered together in factories with large power-driven machines, but generally worked with hand tools or human-powered machines such as spinning wheels or looms in small workshops that were part of their own or someone else's home. They bought the raw materials for whatever they made—leather for shoes, gold for jewelry, flour for bread—and then made the product from start to finish, selling it from their shop or at a city market. Everyone who lived in the house—husband, wife, children, servants, and perhaps some younger people living there as apprentices or trainees—worked on or helped sell the product. In wealthier families, the boys might have some formal schooling, but most children learned their skills from their parents, or from individuals their parents had chosen as their master or instructor.

The parents of eight-year-old Marguerite Cervay apprenticed her for 16 years to a maker of plumed hats, according to an apprenticeship contract from Paris written in 1610. Her master "promised to show her his craft," provide her with "drink, food, fire, bed, home, light, and to treat her gently." She in turn swore that she would "learn the said craft to the best of her ability, without taking flight." If she did run away, her parents swore that they would "search for her in the city and outskirts of Paris and bring her back to finish her service."

An illustration from an early printed book about how to raise children shows an urban family working together. The mother—who is rocking an infant's cradle with her foot—teaches her daughter to spin, while the father teaches a young son to do math, using a book and a counting tool.

No one of the trade of spur-makers shall work longer than from the beginning of the day until curfew rings out [at night] for no man can work so neatly by night as by day... and they [could] practice deception... No one in the spur-makers' trade shall take an apprentice for a shorter term than seven years.

—Regulations for spur-makers in London, 1345

The most desirable neighborhood in the city, with the houses of the wealthiest merchants and government officials, was the center. Slightly out from the center were the houses of craftsmen, often built right onto the next house, making long rows of connected houses. Houses outside the city walls in the suburbs were for poor people and new immigrants, or for people whose occupations were smelly or increased the danger of fire, such as leather-tanners or brick-makers.

To our modern noses, the center of the city would be just as stinky as the suburbs. Especially in European cities, trash was thrown on the street, where pigs and other animals ate it, and animal droppings stayed where they fell. As cities became more crowded, latrines and outhouses filled up and overflowed. When Hernán Cortés and other Spanish conquerors came into the Aztec capital of Tenochtitlan, they were particularly impressed by how clean the city was, and how good it smelled compared to European cities. This was primarily because human and animal waste, and most other garbage, was taken away from the city by canoe.

Along with animals and trash, city streets were filled with servants hurrying to and fro. Most families had at least one live-in servant, and in some cities a quarter of the population was servants. Children might begin service when they were as young as seven or eight, traveling from their home village to a nearby town, and depending on friends and relatives to find them a position. Some of those "servants" were actually slaves—girls from eastern Europe were slaves in Venice, men and women from Africa were slaves in Lisbon in Portugal, young people from the countryside were slaves in Beijing and Istanbul. There was rarely enough room for servants or slaves to have separate quarters, so they generally ate and slept, as well as worked, with the family.

Large numbers of people in any city were very, very poor. They lived in attics or cellars, in rooms they shared, in flimsy housing just inside or just outside city walls, or on the streets. They supported themselves any way they could: gathering and selling firewood, cooking and selling simple things such as eggs or noodle dishes, making soap, trading in used clothing and household articles, or working in taverns, inns, and shops. Men repaired houses and walls, dug ditches, and hauled goods from ships; women did laundry, spun thread, and cared for invalids; children carried messages or packages around the city or the surrounding countryside.

Everyone in the family tried to find something that would bring in money, but often this was not enough. Baron Waldstein only tells us that the thieves and robbers he watched were on their way to be executed, leaving us free to imagine whether they had stolen cloth from a shop, cut the strings on a money-pouch, or grabbed a candlestick from a house. Cities offered great delights and opportunities, but they also offered great temptations, as rich and poor lived only a short walk apart.

Carved doorposts flank the front door of a 16th-century French house. Wealthy city residents in Europe embellished the outside of their homes with stained-glass windows, balconies, sculpture, decorative tiles, and carvings.

CHAPTER 9

SILK AND SPICES

TRAVEL AND TRADE IN THE MEDITERRANEAN SEA AND THE INDIAN OCEAN

"Zheng He and his deputy," wrote the official historian of China's Ming dynasty in the seventeenth century, "as ordered by the emperor, proceeded with their journey to the Western Ocean. Well furnished with treasure and accompanied by more than 27,800 officers and men, they sailed in sixty-two giant ships." The largest of these ships was more than 500 feet long and 150 feet wide, which made it bigger than a football field. The ships sailed southward from a river near the modern city of Shanghai "with sails full-blown" down the coast of Southeast Asia and into the India Ocean, where they "visited one country after another." Admiral Zheng He's expeditions reached the Philippines, the east coast of Africa, and the Arabian Peninsula.

Early Chinese warships were powered by oars as well as sails, and steered from the back of the boat by a large wooden rudder, as the sailor at the right in this 16th-century woodcut is doing. Warships accompanied Zheng He's huge treasure ships on their ocean voyages, and patrolled the South China Sea for pirates and smugglers.

Each fleet included more than 50 ships. Many of these were gigantic treasure ships, designed to carry thousands of soldiers, hundreds of passengers, and huge amounts of cargo. Wherever they landed, Chinese officials "read the imperial decree that demanded the submission of the kingdoms they visited and rewarded generously those rulers who agreed to submit." To those who welcomed him, Zheng He offered Chinese silk, porcelain, and other expensive gifts. "As for those who chose not to obey, force was used to assure their compliance," wrote the Ming historian. Zheng He rarely had to use his soldiers, though, because the impressive sight of the Chinese ships and their crews alone caused people throughout the Indian Ocean basin, and wherever else Zheng He sailed, to submit.

In 1407, two years after he had set off, Zheng He returned to China with officials "from the kingdoms he had visited," who came to pay their respects to the emperor and bring him gifts. "The emperor was greatly pleased and granted titles and financial rewards to all of those who had been presented to him." Zheng He himself gave the emperor exotic treasures and "many prisoners of war," including the captured king of Palembang, part of modern Indonesia.

Zheng He's first expedition was such a success that the Ming emperor who sponsored it, known as the Yongle emperor, sent five more under his command. On one of these expeditions, Zheng He's treasures included a live giraffe brought carefully back from Africa. After the Yongle emperor died, the next emperor sent Zheng He on a seventh voyage. All these expeditions were designed to convince people of Chinese power, gain control over foreign trade with China, and remind Chinese who lived overseas that they owed the emperor taxes. We don't know very much about Admiral Zheng He himself, though we do know he was a Muslim from southwestern China. His voyages allowed him to visit the Muslim holy places of Mecca and Medina, which all Muslims hoped to do sometime in their lives.

A giraffe that Zheng He brought back to China from Africa greatly impressed the imperial court. Caring for the animal on the long voyage was difficult, but sailors had long experience keeping horses, pigs, goats, and sheep alive aboard their ships.

The size of Zheng He's fleet, and the size of the ships in it, were certainly impressive, but the Chinese admiral was not sailing off into unknown waters. Chinese, Indian, Arabic, Persian, and Malay boats had crossed the Indian Ocean and the South China Sea for thousands of years, carrying all types of cargo. By the time of the Renaissance in Europe, this trading network extended to the Mediterranean Sea, with Turkish and Italian ships added to the mix. Buyers, sellers, bankers, sailors, captains, navigators, and people of all types seeking their fortune came together in bustling

The People Are All Rich

MA HUAN, THE OVERALL SURVEY OF THE OCEAN'S SHORES, 1451

Ma Huan was a Chinese Muslim who joined Zheng He's fourth voyage as an Arabic translator. He kept a journal of the trip, and later expanded his notes into a book. He went along again on the sixth and seventh expeditions as well, and combined his journals from all three trips into a longer book, The Overall Survey of the Ocean's Shores, *which he published in 1451. One of the many places he described was the port city of Hormuz in the Persian Gulf.*

Setting sail... you go towards the north-west; and you reach this place after sailing with a fair wind for twenty-five days. The capital lies behind the sea and up against the mountains.

Foreign ships from every place and foreign merchants traveling by land all come to this country to attend the market and trade; hence the people are all rich....

The king of this country, too, took a ship and loaded it with lions, qilin [a giraffe], horses, pearls, precious stones, and other things, and also a memorial to the throne written on a golden leaf; and he sent his chiefs and other men, who accompanied the treasure ships dispatched by the Emperor, which were returning from the Western Ocean [Indian Ocean]; and they went to the capital and presented tribute.

Ma Huan also wrote about the pepper trade in western India.

As to the pepper: the inhabitants of the mountainous countryside have established gardens, and it is extensively cultivated. When the period of the tenth moon arrives, the pepper ripens; [and] it is collected, dried in the sun, and sold. Of course, big pepper-collectors come and collect it, and take it up to the official storehouse to be stored; if there is a buyer, an official gives permission for the sale; the duty [that is, the sales tax] is calculated according to the amount of the purchase price and is paid in to the authorities. Each one po-ho [a measure of weight] is sold for two hundred gold coins.

port cities from Venice, in the west, to Hangzhou, in the east. You could often hear more than 50 languages as you walked through their crowded streets. Merchants and the investors who backed them could become fabulously wealthy if their voyages succeeded, and everyone wanted to get in on the action.

The seas and oceans became busy with the traffic of merchant vessels, and these ships traveled along established routes. Why were sea routes so important? In the long span of human history before trucks and trains, trade by land followed dirt cart-tracks and footpaths. Sheep, horses, and cattle could walk to markets to be sold, but all other merchandise had to be carried, which was difficult and expensive. Powerful empires sometimes built wider roads, occasionally even paved with stones, to allow their armies to move from place to place more easily. Merchants and traders could also use these roads, but most did not last very long. When empires fell apart, their roads were not maintained and they disintegrated, especially because people used them as a

Persian merchants struggle to load a sack on a camel. Large camel caravans regularly traveled the silk roads across Central Asia, but paying for the animals, herders, and guards made transport very expensive.

handy source of stones for building or repairing houses. Rains washed away what was left of the road, and potholes grew so large that people and horses could drown in them.

Because of the danger and the expense, most goods that traveled by land were luxuries rather than basic necessities. The most profitable land route in the world was what became known as the "silk roads" from eastern China to the Mediterranean. Along this route, horse and camel caravans carried Chinese silk, Indian pearls and jewels, and Southeast Asian spices westward, and Italian glassware, central European silver, and northern European amber eastward. (Amber is fossilized sap from pine trees, which sometimes contains insects trapped as the resins flowed from the trees. The translucent orange or yellow pieces look like jewels, but because they can burn and become electrically charged people often regarded amber as magical. The word electricity comes from the Greek word for amber, *elektron.*)

Merchants generally specialized in one leg of the journey, which took months or even years to complete. Each merchant added transport and handling costs to the merchandise. Thus by the time foreign luxuries reached their destinations, they were so expensive that only very wealthy people could afford them. Imports were such a mark of status that even rich people might spend more on them than they could really afford.

One way to reduce the cost of luxury goods was to develop sources closer to home, and silk was a likely candidate for local manufacture. Silk is made from the cocoons of caterpillars called silkworms, which are unwound and then twisted into thread. It is the strongest and most elastic of all natural fibers, warmer than cotton, lighter than wool, and rich-looking when dyed. Silk was discovered in China more than five thousand years ago, and the Chinese guarded the techniques of raising silkworms and making silk thread very carefully. In the 6th century, monks and probably other individuals from the eastern Roman (also called the Byzantine) Empire stole silkworms and the seeds for mulberry trees—the only food that cultivated silkworms will eat—from China. They carried the caterpillars and seeds back to Constantinople in their long, hollow walking sticks.

Silk made in Byzantine cities was traded by land and sea all over the Mediterranean area. Like their Chinese counterparts, the Byzantine emperors tried to stop any further spread of silk-making technology, but this proved impossible. Muslim merchants brought silkworms to Spain and Sicily in the 800s and 900s, and Christian merchants took them to northern Italy by the 1200s and to southern France by the 1500s. Investors even tried to develop silk production in England and Germany, but the winters were too harsh for silkworms.

Though silk could never be produced locally in England or Germany, Byzantine and Italian silk became nearly as good as Chinese, and certainly much cheaper. Wealthy people throughout Europe could afford more silk clothing. Silk thread was used to make very luxurious fabrics such as velvets, brocades, and satins. Clothing styles in the 16th century often included many layers of fancy silk, with slashes cut in the top layers so that the bright colors of the layers underneath showed through. Silk stockings were especially popular, as they clung to—and so showed off—men's and women's legs better than cotton or wool ones.

In a painting from the side of a Ming Dynasty vase, women unwind silk from cocoons while a toddler plays at their feet. Unwinding silk cocoons was a very delicate task, done on sheltered porches or indoors so that the fine threads would not blow away, and it was seen as proper work for women.

Young noblemen wore shorter and shorter shirts and jackets over their stockings to show off their legs, and sometimes these tops were so short that pastors and older officials thought they were too revealing. Many cities in Europe were so concerned that they passed what are called sumptuary laws. Sumptuary laws were sort of like dress codes issued by the city government. They forbade short jackets on men, low necklines on women, and clothing that was too expensive on everyone. They divided city residents

This 14th-century brass astrolabe, a two-dimensional model of the skies, includes a round plate engraved with the hours and the major constellations. Its movable rings could be adjusted to make different calculations. Arabic and European navigators used astrolabes to determine their location and the time of day or night by the position of the sun or stars.

by social class, so that nobles were allowed to wear fur, velvet, and pearls; middle-class people colored wool and cheaper jewelry; and lower-class people only rough cotton or linen and no jewelry or silk, even if they had been given them as gifts.

Along with silk, spices were the most important luxury carried along the silk roads. Spices—pepper, cloves, nutmeg, mace, cardamom, cinnamon, and ginger—served not only as flavoring for food, but also as ingredients in perfumes, love potions, and painkillers. In an era before refrigeration, spices also helped preserve meats and masked the taste of meat that was slightly spoiled. The best spices came from the lands and islands of south and Southeast Asia, some of which became known as the "Spice Islands." (These islands are now called the Moluccas, and are part of Indonesia.) Spices, which require tropical climates to grow, could not be produced in Europe, so the best way to reduce the cost of spices was to reduce the cost of transporting them. The best way to do this was to carry them by water. Even a small ship can carry many times the cargo of a pack animal or cart, and wind can provide the power needed to move that cargo.

A SAKK OF RICHES

Arab and Persian sailors adapted inventions that had been developed in many parts of the world to make their voyages safer and easier. They used simple magnetic compasses—either a magnetized needle laid on a floating wood chip or a pivoting needle on a compass card—that were invented in

China. They used metal astrolabes, flat disks with hands that could be turned, invented in the Mediterranean for observing and calculating the positions of planets and stars in the night sky. These measurements were used for figuring latitude, the distance north or south from the equator. Compasses and astrolabes helped sailors find their position on the high seas. The triangle-shaped lateen sail, invented in India, made their ships more maneuverable and allowed them to sail more directly against the wind on round-trip voyages than with traditional square sails.

Along with these technical developments, the spread of Islam in the Near East and south Asia beginning in the 7th century encouraged trade. Islamic law includes provisions about contracts and other business issues, so merchants could count on the same laws applying wherever they bought and sold merchandise. Muslim merchants gradually brought parts of Africa into this trading network, and made huge fortunes in business and banking. The modern banking word "check," in fact, comes from the Arabic word *sakk*.

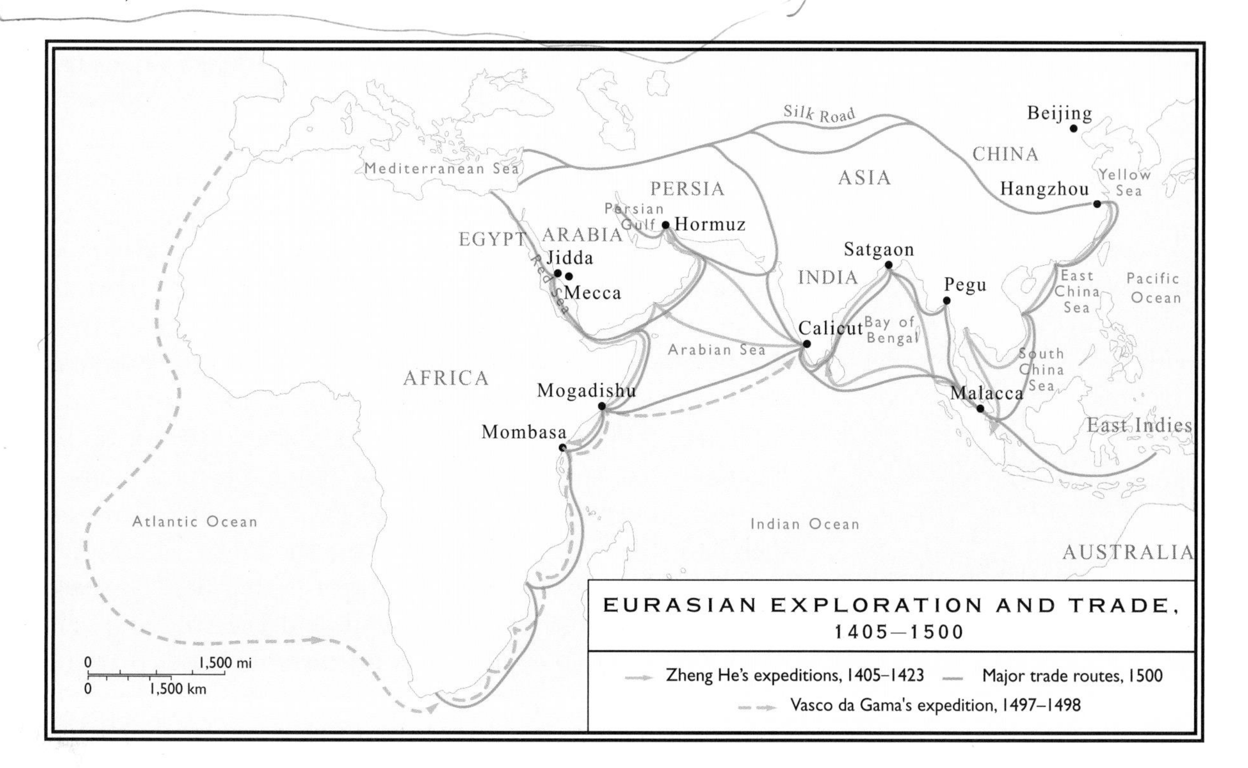

EURASIAN EXPLORATION AND TRADE, 1405–1500

Two Indian jewel merchants bargain over pearls and other gems. India exported many jewels such as rubies and sapphires, which were not only used for necklaces, pins, and earrings, but also as substitutes for money.

A *sakk* was a letter that a merchant could take from one city to another, which said that he had deposited money with a business in the first city. (Banks developed as places to keep money only later.) When he got to the second city, the merchant could buy things with this letter, because the people trading with him knew they could collect what was owed them from the business where his money was deposited. Most business at this time was done in gold, silver, and copper coins, and the *sakk* meant that the merchant did not have to carry a heavy cash box. Like a modern check, the *sakk* was also more secure than cash, as the merchant to whom it was issued was the only one who could use it.

Indian, Arab, Malay, Persian, and Turkish merchants, many of them Muslim, controlled the trade in spices and other luxuries in Asia and the Near East. Once goods got to Cairo or Constantinople, European merchants, most of whom were Christian, often handled them. The majority of these merchants came from northern Italian cities such as Venice, Genoa, Pisa, and Florence.

These Italian merchants developed new ways of doing business that spread the risks of doing business among investors and kept better track of their ventures. Venetian merchants set up permanent offices in Cairo, where they dealt in spices that were traded up the Red Sea. Genoese merchants went to Constantinople and the shores of the Black Sea, where they met caravans carrying goods over the silk roads. (A Genoese ship may have carried the first wave of the plague from a port on the Black Sea to Europe in

The doge [the ruler of Venice] celebrates a festival each year before the harbor on the high seas. He then throws a golden finger ring into the wild sea, as a sign that he takes the sea to wife, as one who intends to be lord over the whole sea.

—German merchant Arnold von Harff, reporting in his journal on a festival in Venice, 1497

1347.) A few Italians went to the coastal cities of western India. These cities were becoming cosmopolitan mixtures of Hindus, Buddhists, Muslims, Jews, and Christians, all intent on making the best business deals. Some Italians went even further. The Venetian merchant Marco Polo spent 17 years at the court of Khublai Khan in China in the late 13th century.

Wherever they came from and wherever they went, merchants bought and sold slaves along with their other merchandise. Italian merchants bought young women in Russia and North Africa to be household slaves in Venice, Genoa, and other Mediterranean cities. Spanish and Portuguese merchants bought North African men captured in war, and sold them to European navies as galley slaves to row merchant vessels and warships. Turkish merchants bought Russians, Ukrainians, and Poles who had been captured in eastern Europe, and sold them as household slaves, soldiers, textile workers, and servants in the sultan's palace.

Dockworkers unload a merchant ship in a European port, while more ships wait their turn in the background. The docks and wharves of port cities were bustling places filled with sailors and traders from many parts of the world.

The island is visited by many ships from various parts of the world, bringing assortments of goods consisting of brocades and silks of various patterns, which are sold to the merchants of the island, or bartered for goods in return. They make large profits.

—The Venetian traveler and merchant Marco Polo, writing about the island of Madagascar on the East African coast in *Description of the World,* 1298

Arabic and African merchants crossed the Sahara Desert in both directions with slaves—West Africans going to the Mediterranean and eastern Europeans going to West Africa. Indian and Arabic merchants bought slaves in the coastal regions of East Africa, taking them to the west coast of India or further eastward. Because they were often taken far from home, slaves in many places were outsiders. They differed from their owners in terms of religion, language, or physical appearance. Owners were usually legally forbidden from killing their slaves, and religious teachings advised them to treat their slaves kindly, but in no part of the world was slavery itself seen as wrong.

By the 15th century, people who had been on the fringes of the Indian Ocean–Mediterranean trading network became more active. When Zheng He was making his expeditions, it seemed as if China might come to dominate trade in the Indian Ocean. However, after Zheng He died, support at the Chinese court for such voyages ended. Later emperors worried more about attacks from the Mongols on China's northwestern border than about overseas expeditions. They sent large armies and greatly extended the Great Wall of China to defend against these attacks.

All this cost money, and Zheng He's expeditions had cost more than they brought back. The emperors' officials decided they were too expensive, so they destroyed almost all Zheng He's maps and logbooks so that voyages like his would not be attempted in the future. (A few survived, and historians in China today are using them to find out more about Zheng He's voyages.) Chinese merchants continued to trade all over the South China Sea, but Zheng He's huge ships rotted away. The Chinese emperors did not attempt to exert naval power again.

THE NAVIGATOR PRINCE SENDS SHIPS SAILING

At almost the same time that the Yongle emperor was sending Zheng He on his voyages, the third son of the king in a tiny country on the far western end of the Mediterranean also decided to increase his country's influence. Prince Henry of Portugal, later dubbed Prince Henry the Navigator, sponsored Portuguese explorations down the West African coast and military expeditions against Muslim forces in North Africa.

When Henry was only 21, he and his navy conquered the Muslim port city of Ceuta in Morocco, and he became its governor. He learned about the land routes between Ceuta and central Africa, but thought that, in the words of the Portuguese *Chronicle of the Discovery and Conquest of Guinea*, written in 1453, "many kinds of merchandise might be brought to this realm" more easily by sea, which "would bring great profit to our countrymen." It might also allow the Portuguese to connect with a Christian kingdom they erroneously believed to exist south of the Sahara Desert, which might "aid him against those enemies of the faith," the Muslims. "It was his great desire to make increase in the faith of our Lord Jesus Christ," reports the chronicler, "by which his spirit may be glorified after this life in the celestial realm," that is, in heaven.

Portuguese ships inched farther and farther down the African coast. The way that the winds normally blew in the Atlantic meant that although ships could stick close to land when sailing south, they had to cut far to the west when sailing home to Portugal. Because of these routes, Portuguese sailors found islands in the Atlantic, including the Azores, Cape Verde, and Madeira. Here Henry encouraged colonization and farming, especially raising sugar cane. One of Henry's explorers brought the first slaves from West

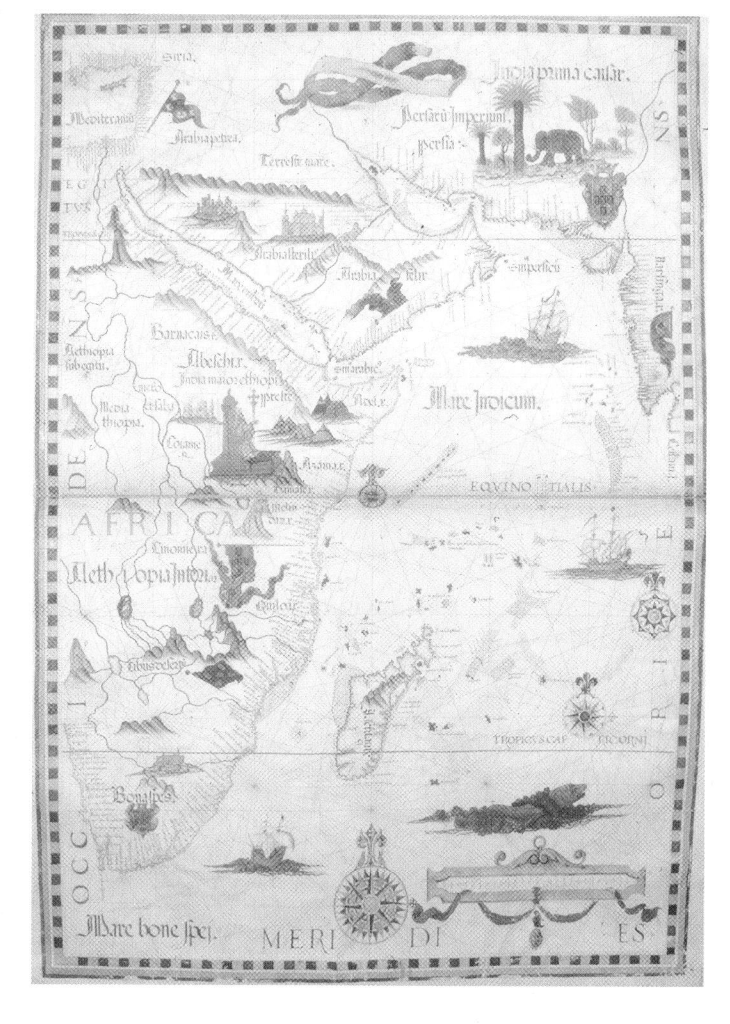

A detailed and very accurate Portuguese map of the east coast of Africa and the west coast of India, made in 1558. Portuguese rulers supported mapmakers, astronomers, and mathematicians, all of whom made charts, maps, and calculations to assist ships' captains.

Armor-clad Portuguese men with guns and daggers surround a leopard on this West African plaque from the 17th century. African artists often included in their paintings and sculpture images of the Europeans who traded along the African coast.

Africa to Europe in 1441. From these Africans, Henry learned more about lands farther south than his ships had sailed.

In the 1450s a Genoese merchant under Henry's sponsorship made direct contact with the Songhay Empire of West Africa. With this contact, trade increased dramatically. Europeans traded guns, cloth, and other manufactured goods for African gold and slaves. A few of these West African slaves, who had been captured in raids or sold into slavery, went to Europe as household slaves, dock workers, or farm laborers. Most of them, however, went to the sugar plantations of the new Portuguese colonies on the Atlantic Islands.

The king then asked, if he came to discover men, why had he brought nothing?... [Then he said:] My country is rich in cinnamon, cloves, ginger, pepper, and precious stones. That which I ask of you in exchange is gold, silver, corals, and scarlet cloth.

—The comments of King Camolim, the ruler of a state on the west coast of India, to Vasco da Gama about his first voyage, from an anonymous journal of da Gama's voyage, 1497–99

Portuguese captains continued to press southward in search of more African riches. They were also trying to find a sea route to the Indian Ocean that would allow them to buy spices directly and avoid Arab or Italian middlemen. In 1488, Bartolomeu Dias rounded the southern tip of Africa, but his tired sailors forced him to return to Portugal rather than continuing up the east coast of Africa. In 1497, King Manuel I of Portugal sponsored a fleet of four ships under the command of Vasco da Gama, an experienced sea captain whose father was also a sea captain. These ships were equipped with the best new technology—compasses and astrolabes that the Portuguese had learned about from

Arabic sailors, and astronomical charts developed by Prince Henry's scholars.

Da Gama's ships rounded Africa and sailed up its east coast until they reached towns where they could find mariners with experience in the Indian Ocean. On the east coast of Africa they met "tawny men who have long beards and long hair, which they braid," who "eat no meat," according to a journal of this voyage. Da Gama hired one of these Indians as a ship's pilot, and his little fleet reached Calicut (modern-day Kozhikode) on the west coast of India by sailing directly across the Arabian Sea. Indian and Arabic merchants who were already there resisted da Gama, and he left for Portugal with fewer spices than he had hoped. King Manuel I still rewarded him richly and gave him the title "Admiral of the Indian Ocean."

The king sent da Gama back three years later, this time with 20 warships. Da Gama bombarded Calicut with his cannons, defeated an Indian fleet, and conquered the city. He returned to Portugal with a huge amount of spices, gold, jewels, and other plunder, and the king made him a count. Da Gama was sent to India once more, in 1524, to replace the official in charge of Portuguese territory there, but he died soon after he arrived.

Though da Gama's first voyage had not been a financial success, his later expeditions and Portuguese ventures on the west coast of Africa were very, very profitable. In this they were the opposite of Zheng He's voyages, which lost money. Portuguese rulers had no doubts about whether they should keep sending more. They brought such riches and glory, in fact, that other rulers in Europe decided they should get into the exploration business, too.

The Portuguese ship captain Vasco da Gama was the first European to reach India by sailing around Africa. Da Gama wears an embroidered velvet jacket with the sleeves slashed to show the red silk beneath, just the sort of luxurious clothing that European city leaders tried to prohibit because they thought it was a waste of money.

CHAPTER 10

"COLUMBIA" OR "AMERICA"?

NAMES AND FAME IN A "NEW WORLD"

Columbus and one of his ships sail near the islands of the Caribbean. Fanciful woodcuts like this were printed as illustrations with Columbus's letters and journals.

"In fourteen hundred ninety-two, Columbus sailed the ocean blue," goes the rhyme children learn about Christopher Columbus. In 1992, people marked the 500th anniversary of his first voyage with television specials, parades, and reenactments of the trip. Some of these were happy celebrations, and others emphasized grief, for the anniversary sparked debates about the man himself and the impact of his journeys. Was he a brave explorer, unafraid to sail out of sight of land unlike most people of his time? Or was he a religious fanatic and a racist, convinced that God had called him to fight the power of Islam and to convert people he thought were inferior to Christians, by force if necessary? Did his voyages lead to helpful global exchanges of crops such as corn, potatoes, rice, chocolate, and coffee? Or did they instead bring devastation, as European diseases such as smallpox and measles killed millions of people in the Americas?

The answer is probably "yes" to all these questions, so the argument is more complicated than whether Columbus was a good guy or a bad guy. People who study Columbus also agree on several other things: He was not the first European to cross the Atlantic. He was an enthusiastic reader of books by earlier travelers and books on geography and astronomy written by ancient Greeks and Egyptians. Those books, and the practical experience of sailors, had taught people that the world was round.

Vikings crossed the Atlantic to Greenland and Canada in ships similar to this one. They sailed the chilly and stormy waters in boats that were completely open to the weather, but very seaworthy.

When he was young, Columbus lived in port cities of Italy, Spain, and Portugal, where sailors, ships' pilots, and captains all told about their travels in the Indian Ocean and down the coast of Africa. In these port cities, he also gained practical knowledge about shipbuilding, navigation, and guns.

The first Europeans who crossed the Atlantic were Vikings. These seafaring northern people described their voyages to the west in sagas—long poems about heroes and gods—but until 1960 most people thought the sagas were just myths. Humans leave things wherever they go, however, and in the 1960s Norwegian archeologists found the remains of Viking houses, boat sheds, cooking pits, and garbage heaps on the island of Newfoundland in Canada. This was probably an outpost colony from the Viking settlements on Iceland and Greenland, and may have been inhabited for only a few decades around the year 1000.

Greenland itself is often described as the first real-estate scam, because the Viking leader Erik the Red gave it that name to attract settlers from snowy Norway, even though there was very little green in sight. There were also no large trees in Greenland, so the Vikings continued to go to Canada for wood after the colony there had disbanded. In the 14th century, the climate turned colder and the Greenland settlers all died of starvation. The plague reached Iceland in the early 15th century, carried by trading ships just as it had been carried into Italy, and the number of voyages in the north Atlantic declined. Stories told about westward voyages seemed just that—stories, not history—to the Icelandic survivors of the plague and to anyone else who heard them.

Columbus did not read the Viking accounts, but he did read those of many other travelers, including Marco Polo, whose writings were easily available in printed versions. Some of the actual books Columbus took with him on his voyages have survived, and you can see his handwritten notes in the margins. One of these was the newly published book of geography by the ancient Greek scholar Ptolemy, which gave estimates for the size of the earth that we now know were much too small, and estimates for the size of Asia that we know were too large.

Columbus's understanding of the world did not come just from books. He was the son of a weaver, with little formal schooling, but he taught himself to read several languages once he was an adult. He grew up in the bustling Italian port city of Genoa, where hanging around the docks he could listen to mariners and merchants who had traveled the Mediterranean, the Indian Ocean, and beyond. The barrels of wine, crates of silk, bags of spices, and kegs of oil piled up on the Genoese docks showed him the riches that trade could bring, and he joined the crew of a merchant ship when he was a teenager. When he was in his 20s, he settled in Lisbon, Portugal, with his brother, making maps to support himself. He married a woman whose father was one of Henry the Navigator's captains and a governor of Madeira, one of the colonies the Portuguese had set up on the Atlantic Islands. The couple lived on Madeira for a while, and Columbus visited many other islands and the Portuguese trading posts on the west coast of Africa.

In Portugal, Columbus also got to know the group of geographers and astronomers whom Henry the Navigator had brought together. From his reading and his conversations, he developed a new plan for obtaining Asian silks and

A globe made in 1543 is set within an armillary sphere, a model of the universe in which the paths of the planets are shown as rings designed to help teach geography and astronomy. This globe shows North America and Asia as connected, and its rings place the earth in the center of the universe. Later voyages and astronomical discoveries showed both ideas to be wrong.

spices—sail westward rather than around Africa. He combined Ptolemy's ideas of the size of the world and the size of Asia, Marco Polo's estimations of how far he had traveled in China, and several other sources to calculate that the distance from the Canary Islands—the most western European colony—to Japan was only 2,500 miles. This was a long, but doable, journey, especially in the new types of ships the Portuguese were already using in the south Atlantic.

These ships, called caravels, carried several different types of sails: large and small square sails for speed when the wind was from the rear, and triangular, or lateen, sails, for use when there was a crosswind from the side. Their captains and pilots also used compasses and astrolabes to figure out their location, and had devised various ways for measuring speed, such as timing how fast wood chips floated by the ship. These tools for navigation were not very accurate, but in experienced hands they allowed mariners to feel secure in sailing far out of sight of land.

Columbus took his plan to sail westward to the most likely backers, the Portuguese court, where the king's council firmly rejected it. They knew that almost all trained astronomers and geographers agreed that Ptolemy had greatly underestimated the size of the earth, and that Marco

The country was flat and covered with forest, with extensive white sands wherever they went.... There was no lack of salmon there in the river or lake, and salmon bigger than they had ever seen before.

—Viking description of Canada, from *The Greenlanders' Saga*, 13th century

A replica of Columbus's flagship Santa Maria *was built for 1992 Columbus Day celebrations and now sits on the river in Columbus, Ohio. The* Santa Maria *was wider and clumsier than Columbus's other two ships, and after it became hopelessly stuck on Hispaniola (modern-day Haiti), he had it taken apart and used the timber to build a fort.*

Polo had exaggerated his journeys. The distance from Europe to Asia going westward was much longer than Columbus proposed, and a voyage taking this route would be far too costly.

Columbus next tried the Spanish court, where for many years he got the same reaction, and for the same reasons: his calculations were wrong, and it was too expensive. The Spanish monarchs, Isabella and Ferdinand, were intensely religious, however, and grew more interested once Columbus told them he planned to use the wealth gained from his trip to recapture Jerusalem from the Muslims. He told them he was destined by God to spread Christianity, a destiny symbolized by his first name, Christo-fero, which means "Christ carrier" in Latin. (Columbus often signed his first name using the Greek symbol for Christ.)

In 1492, Spanish armies conquered Granada, the last Muslim territory in Spain, and the Spanish monarchs banished the Jews from their realm. Isabella and Ferdinand

Columbus arrives at the court of Isabella and Ferdinand, in a dramatic scene with fur-clad courtiers in attendance and the royal fool at the feet of the monarchs. Writers, artists, and movie-makers have sometimes suggested that there was romance between Columbus and Isabella, but there is no evidence of this.

wanted to continue expanding Christianity, and also find a way to keep Spanish soldiers busy. Several weeks after Granada was defeated, Columbus received the support of Queen Isabella, and later that year he left Spain with three ships and about 90 crew members. He carried Chinese silk in his sea chests, figuring that wherever he landed, people would know about this beautiful fabric and could direct him to where it was made. He also brought along an Arabic-speaking Spaniard as a translator, figuring that with all the trade around the Indian Ocean and South China Sea, someone at the Chinese court certainly spoke Arabic.

THE NEW WORLD—NO GOLD, BUT PLENTY OF FISH

About five weeks after setting sail from the Canary Islands, Columbus's ships landed at an island in the Caribbean, which he named San Salvador, Spanish for Holy Savior. He was certain that he had reached an island off Asia, and called the inhabitants, who were members of the Taino people, "Indians," because he thought he was in the Indies, a word Europeans used for the islands of Southeast Asia. (The islands where Columbus landed were later called the West Indies, and those of Southeast Asia the East Indies.) Looking for Japan or the Asian mainland, he explored numerous islands for several months, then set off again for Spain, taking several captured Tainos with him. After a rough voyage, he was greeted in triumph by Isabella and Ferdinand, and immediately began preparations for a return voyage.

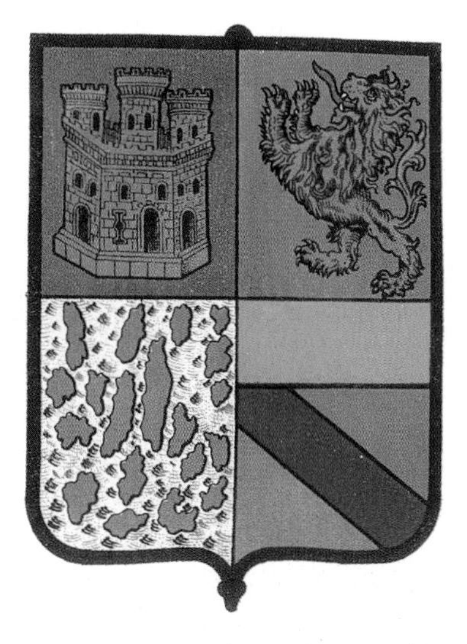

Columbus's coat of arms features the symbols of Aragon and Castile in the top half, and islands and anchors below. Isabella and Ferdinand granted Columbus this symbol of his right to bear arms, a privilege usually limited to nobles, as a reward for his service.

This second voyage was very different from the first—17 ships, crowded with more than a thousand men, including priests who wished to convert the Indians to Christianity and colonists intending to settle on the islands, but mostly men looking for easy riches. They were sadly disappointed, and many went home again after only a few weeks. Columbus and his brothers governed different island colonies, never very successfully. Spanish colonists

continues on page 144

All These Islands Are Very Beautiful

CHRISTOPHER COLUMBUS, LETTER TO QUEEN ISABELLA AND KING FERDINAND, 1493

Columbus wrote this letter to Queen Isabella and King Ferdinand on the way back from his first voyage, while stopping in the Azores Islands. He sent the letter from Lisbon, so that it would arrive at the Spanish court right before he got there. It was published in Spanish, the language in which he wrote it, in 1493, and then in many other European languages. It formed the basis of many Europeans' impressions of the "New World."

I have decided upon writing this letter to acquaint you with all the events which have occurred in my voyage, and the discoveries which have resulted from it. Thirty-three days after my departure from Cadiz I reached the Indian sea, where I discovered many islands, thickly peopled. Of which I took possession without resistance in the name of our most illustrious Monarchs, by public proclamation and with unfurled banners. To the first of these islands, which is called by the Indians Guanahani, I gave the name of the blessed Savior (San Salvador), relying upon whose protection I had reached this as well as the other islands. . . .

Caribbean people paddle a large wooden canoe designed with a canopy to protect them from the sun. Sturdy multi-paddler canoes allowed people to travel easily from island to island.

All these islands are very beautiful, and distinguished by a diversity of scenery; they are filled with a great variety of trees of immense height. . . . There are very extensive fields and meadows, a variety of birds, different kinds of honey, and many sorts of metals, but no iron. . . . The inhabitants of these islands . . . carry however, instead of [fire]arms, canes dried in the sun, on the ends of which they fix heads of dried wood sharpened to a point. . . . They practice no kind of idolatry, but have a firm belief that all strength and power, and indeed all good things, are in heaven. . . .

On my arrival, I had taken some Indians by force from the first island that I came to, in order that they might learn our language and communicate what they knew respecting the country; which plan succeeded excellently, and was a great advantage to us, for in a short time, either by gestures and signs, or by words, we were enabled to understand each other. . . .

Each of these islands has a great number of canoes, built of solid wood, narrow and not unlike our double-hulled boats in length and shape, but swifter in their motion: they steer them only by the oar. . . The greater number are constructed with eighteen banks of oars, and with these they cross to the other islands, which are of countless number, to carry on traffic with the people. I saw some of these canoes that held as many as seventy-eight rowers.

In all these islands there is no difference in physiognomy [outward facial appearance], of manners, or of language, but they all clearly understand each other, a circumstance very propitious [fortunate] for the realization of what I conceive to be the principal wish of our most serene King, namely, the conversion of these people to the holy faith of Christ, to which indeed, as far as I can judge, they are very favorable and well-disposed. . . .

There was one large town in Española of which especially I took possession, situated in a remarkably favorable spot, and in every way convenient for the purposes of gain and commerce. To this town I gave the name *Navidad del Señor* [Birth of our Lord], and ordered a fortress to be built there, which must by this time be completed, in which I left as many men as I thought necessary with all sorts of arms, and enough provisions for more than a year. I left them one caravel, and skillful workmen both in ship-building and other arts. . . .

I could not clearly understand whether the people possess any private property, for I observed that one man had charge of distributing various things to the rest, but especially meat and provisions and the like. I did not find, as some of us had expected, any cannibals among them, but on the contrary men of great deference and kindness.

continued from page 141

complained that food was scarce and work too hard. The Tainos and other Indians died from European diseases or the harsh treatment they received after being made slaves. There was no gold or other riches to be found. Columbus returned to Spain to defend himself, and for his third voyage he found so few willing men that Ferdinand and Isabella had to release prisoners to serve as crew.

On his third voyage, in 1498, he explored what is now the coast of Venezuela, finding the mouth of an enormous river—the Orinoco—which made him realize this had to be a large landmass and not just an island. (Islands do not accumulate enough rainfall to allow large freshwater rivers to form.) He wrote in his journal that he had found a "very great continent... until today unknown," and that God had

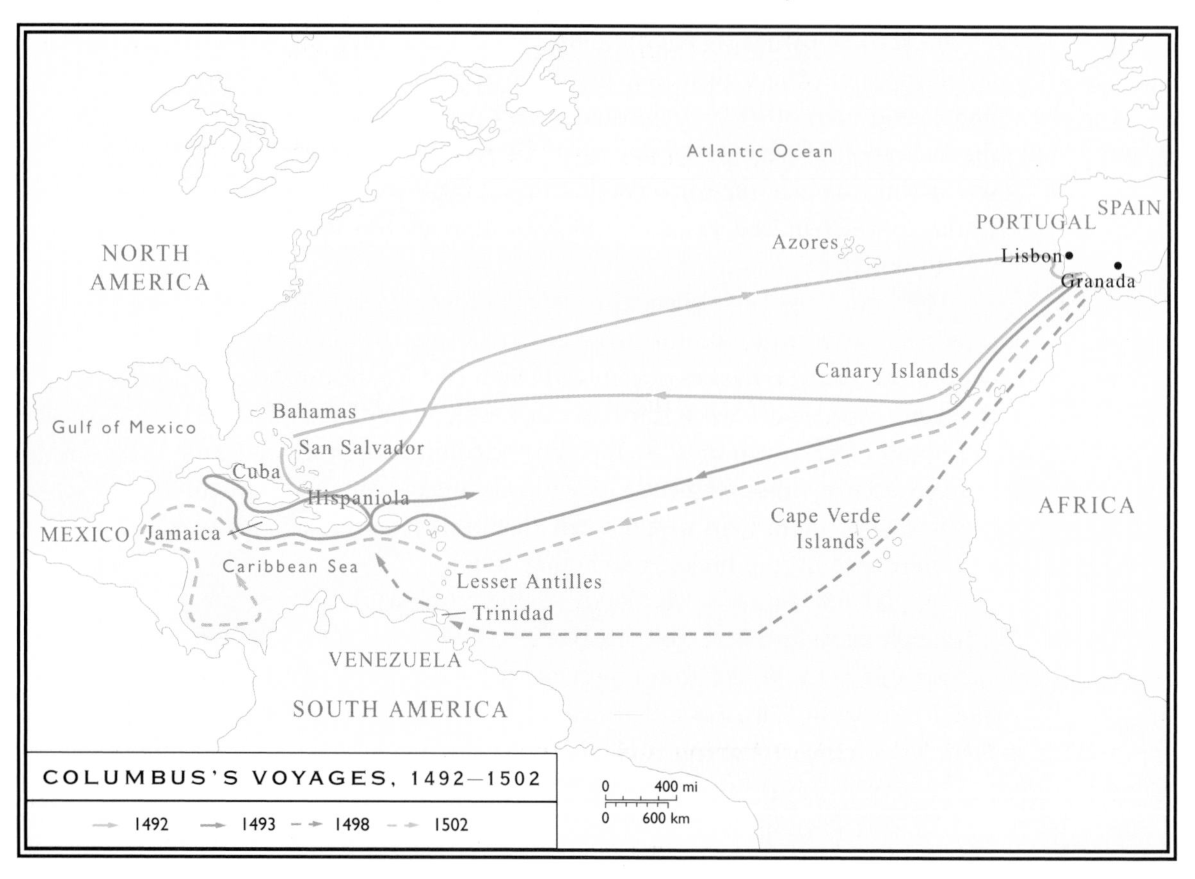

COLUMBUS'S VOYAGES, 1492–1502

made him "the messenger of the new world." This was the first time that he used the words "new world" for what he had found, though he still believed that Asia was just to the west. On his fourth and final voyage, he sailed along the coast of Central America looking for a passage to China, and was then marooned for more than a year on Jamaica. He died in 1506, just two years after returning to Spain for the final time and two years after the death of his strongest supporter, Queen Isabella.

Columbus's own career was not always glorious, but the news of his first voyage spread immediately throughout Europe. The letter that he wrote to Isabella and Ferdinand after his first voyage—sent by messenger from the dock in the Portuguese capital of Lisbon so that it would arrive at their court just before he did—was quickly published, first in Spanish and then in many other languages. Not only were there many volunteers for Columbus's second voyage, but other mariners and adventurers found backers for their own expeditions.

Another young man from Columbus's hometown of Genoa, Giovanni Caboto, followed the same career path that Columbus did. He worked on merchant ships in the Mediterranean, became a mapmaker, and moved westward looking for support for longer voyages. He ended up in England, where he changed his name to the more English-sounding John Cabot. Cabot thought that it would be faster to take a northern route to China, got the backing of King Henry VII of England and merchants in the port city of Bristol, and in 1497 made the first English voyage to North America.

Cabot landed somewhere near where the Viking colony had been, on the bleak and rocky shore of Canada. Like Columbus, he found no gold or treasure, and he left no journal of his voyage, so we don't even know exactly where he landed. An English merchant writing to Columbus the same year reported that Cabot "had a disagreement with the crew" and "ran short of food," but Cabot himself wrote no letters. He did find the richest fishing area in the world, what was later called the Grand Banks, in Newfoundland. (This area remained an important source of the world's fish

We ask and require that you acknowledge the Church as the Ruler and Superior of the whole world, and the King and Queen as superiors and lords of these islands.... If you do so, we shall leave you your lands.... If you do not, we shall forcibly enter into your country and make war against you.

—Official royal proclamation that Spanish conquerors read aloud (in Spanish) to Indian communities they encountered

Mapmakers named America after Amerigo Vespucci, an Italian merchant and ship's captain who reported in a widely published letter that he had sailed to the coast of South America in 1497, before Columbus. This report is now thought to be completely made up, and his claims to have commanded whole fleets are known to be exaggerated.

for centuries, until it had to be closed because of overfishing in the late 20th century.) His voyage also gave England a claim to the mainland of North America and led to the founding of the English colonies, though Cabot himself disappeared mysteriously on a second voyage.

Amerigo Vespucci was another enterprising Italian. Born in Florence, the wealthy center of Renaissance culture, Vespucci first worked for a banking firm run by the Medici family. He moved to Spain, got involved in overseas trade, and served as a ship's captain on several Spanish and Portuguese voyages to the New World. In 1503, he wrote a letter to his old employers, the Medicis, trumpeting the wonders of the "new world" he had seen, with "much continental land and innumerable islands, and great part of them inhabited." He claimed to have been the first European to see what is now Venezuela on a voyage in 1497, a year before Columbus got there. There, he wrote, he found "people smooth and clean of body," who "are very light footed in walking and running" and "sleep in very large nettings of cotton, suspended in the air."

This letter was published many times in many different languages. The phrase "New World" began to show up on hand-drawn and printed world maps around 1505, and shortly after that the word "America," meaning "the land of Amerigo," also appeared, because mapmakers read and believed Vespucci's letter. By just a few years later, mapmakers and others knew that Columbus had been the first European to arrive in this "new world." They wanted to omit the label "America" from future maps, but the name had already stuck.

Our intention was to take the young girls by force and bring them to Castile as a wonderful thing... [but] there entered as many as thirty-six men. . . .They carried very large bows and arrows... and [we walked] away in the direction of the ship as if nothing had happened.

—Amerigo Vespucci, letter to the Medicis written in 1503, describing his trip to South America in 1497

FINDERS, KEEPERS?

While Spanish and English ships were exploring the coasts of what were becoming known as South America and North America, the Portuguese were as well. In 1500, Bartolomeu Dias, the Portuguese explorer who had first rounded the southern tip of Africa, commanded ships in an expedition led by Pedro Alvares Cabral, another Portuguese adventurer. They were on their way down the West African coast to India, but the fleet drifted off course, and landed in eastern South America. They found trees that were the color of glowing coals, and called both the trees and the country Brazil, after the word for this color in Portuguese, "brasa." The expedition continued on its way, but storms, shipwrecks, and fighting took most of the ships and sailors, including Dias. Despite these disasters, the voyage allowed Portugal to claim Brazil as its colony.

Portugal's claim to eastern South America was supported by an international treaty drawn up several years before Cabral's and Dias's voyage, before anyone in Europe knew that South America was even there. Right after Columbus returned from his first voyage, the rulers of Portugal and Spain realized that their expeditions might lead to disputes over who had rights to certain areas. They appealed to an international authority, the pope, who drew an imaginary line down what he thought was the middle of the Atlantic Ocean, giving Portugal all the newly discovered lands to the

Central American women make tortillas in an illustration titled "Method of making bread" from a History of the New World *published in Italy in 1565. The author had spent many years traveling in Central America and the Caribbean and provided many comments about daily life. Here he describes how the women soak the kernels overnight before grinding them "with two stones."*

east and Spain all those to the west. This Line of Demarcation was moved about 1,000 miles westward the next year in the Treaty of Tordesillas so that it ran right through South America, though no one knew that yet. The pope's division of the globe supported Cabral's claim, and Portugal became the ruler of Brazil, even though a Spanish expedition was exploring the mouth of what they named the Amazon River in the same year.

When the Treaty of Tordesillas was drawn up in 1494, only Portugal and Spain were sponsoring ocean voyages, and according to the terms of the treaty, the Line of Demarcation was continued around the entire world "from pole to pole," which meant the Philippine Islands off the coast of Asia were supposed to belong to Portugal. The first European expedition to land in the Philippines was a Spanish one, however, and in later treaties Portugal agreed to give up the Philippines to Spain in exchange for a larger part of South America.

This 1622 Spanish map clearly indicates the Line of Demarcation dividing the world into Spanish and Portuguese zones. The line drawn in the Atlantic by the pope (the darkest vertical line, cutting through South America) continues around the whole world, cutting through China and putting the Philippines squarely in the Spanish zone.

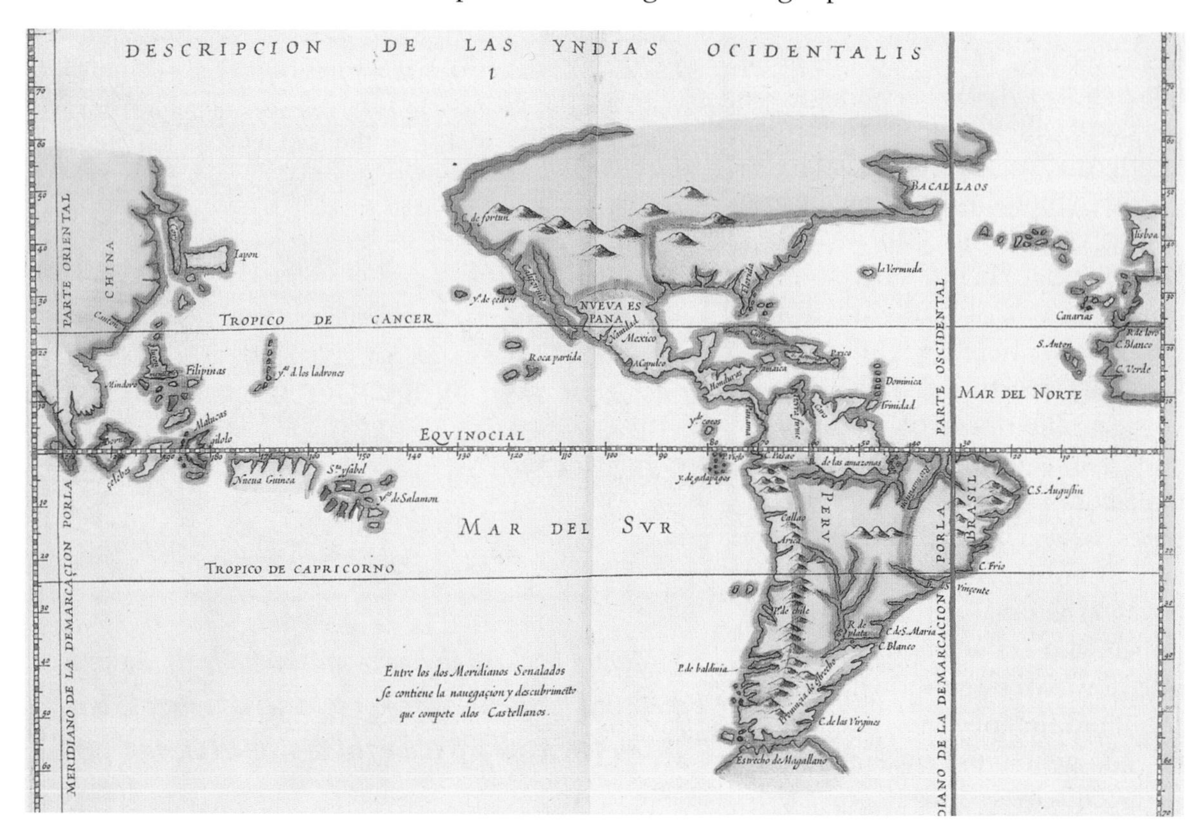

The Spanish expedition to the Philippines was actually led by a Portuguese sea captain, Ferdinand Magellan, who had spent many years sailing around the Indian Ocean, Southeast Asia, and the Spice Islands. Orphaned at age 10, Magellan grew up at the Portuguese royal court, where he learned about navigation and naval warfare, and a battle wound left him with a permanent limp. He tried to convince the king of Portugal to fund a voyage to reach the Spice Islands by sailing west. King Manuel refused, but in 1518, the teenaged king of Spain, Charles I (who ruled from 1516 to 1555, the same man who later became the German Emperor Charles V), agreed to support Magellan. He set off from Spain with five ships, first to Brazil and down the coast of South America to the frigid waters near Antarctica.

When he first saw seals and penguins, Antonio Pigafetta, an Italian adventurer who had paid Magellan to take him along, wrote in his diary: "Coasting along the land, we came to anchor at two islands full of geese and seawolves. Those geese are black. They do not fly, and live on fish. The seawolves have no legs but only feet with small nails attached." During the freezing and stormy trip around the tip of South America, one of Magellan's ships sank and the crew of another mutinied and turned around for home. Magellan finally found a way around the continent, through what is now known as the Straits of Magellan, and gave the ocean into which he sailed the name Pacific, which means peaceful, because it seemed much calmer than the Atlantic.

Magellan's voyage was far from peaceful, however. The Pacific was so huge that the food supply ran out, and the crew boiled their leather bags along with the ships' rats to eat. With no fruits or vegetables, they suffered from scurvy, a disease caused by lack of vitamin C, which made their joints grow sore, their gums bleed, and their teeth fall out. Once in the Philippines, Magellan and some of his crew were attacked when they burned some houses "in order to terrify them [the native Filipinos]." "Recognizing the captain," wrote Pigafetta, "they rushed upon him with iron and bamboo spears, until they killed him, our mirror, our light, our comfort, and our true guide." Only one of Magellan's

The unknown painter of this portrait labeled Ferdinand Magellan as "most famous for having conquered the difficulties of the Antarctic Strait." Magellan was killed on the voyage when he intervened in a battle in the Philippines, and credit for circumnavigating the globe was first given to one of his captains who actually made it back home. But with the publication of the diary of Antonio Pigafetta, a member of the expedition who praised Magellan's courage and skills, the fame and credit shifted to Magellan.

ships, with 18 survivors from the original crew of 240 and several men from the Spice Islands, made it back to Spain.

The pope may have divided the world in a way that satisfied Spain and Portugal, but other European nations were not included. Just a week before Magellan was killed in the Philippines, Martin Luther stood in front of Emperor Charles V, the very same ruler who had backed Magellan, and declared his independence from the pope in matters of religion. Newly Protestant countries such as England and the Netherlands saw no reason to follow the pope's division of the world. On their voyages, they claimed territory they discovered for themselves, and even Catholic countries such as France eventually simply ignored the Line of Demarcation. European claims to territory were based much more on actual voyages, military force, and the establishment of colonies than on imaginary lines drawn by popes.

Most of the land that Columbus and other early European explorers claimed for their own countries already had people living on it, of course. Many of the Atlantic Islands off the coast of Africa were uninhabited, but the Canary Islands had been settled at least 1,500 years before Columbus's time by people called Guanches, who were probably descendents of the earliest inhabitants of North Africa, the herding and farming people known as Berbers. (Sailors gave these islands their name because of the large, fierce dogs—*canis* in Latin—the Guanches used to herd sheep and goats. The birds we call canaries were first found on these islands.) The Caribbean Islands had been settled from the mainland of the Americas, which were themselves populated all the way from the Arctic in the north to the Straits of Magellan in the south. The history of European expansion is therefore a story of conquest as well as exploration and trade.

A 1596 map of the Americas includes images of Columbus, Vespucci, Magellan, and Pizarro, the conqueror of Peru. The mapmaker put a large land mass labeled "terra Australis" at the bottom, but this just means "southern land" in Latin and was there because people thought there had to be something there to balance all the northern continents. The first known European sighting of Australia took place in 1606.

CHAPTER 11

SAILORS, SUGAR, AND SLAVES

HOW EUROPEAN VOYAGES CHANGED ASIA AND AFRICA

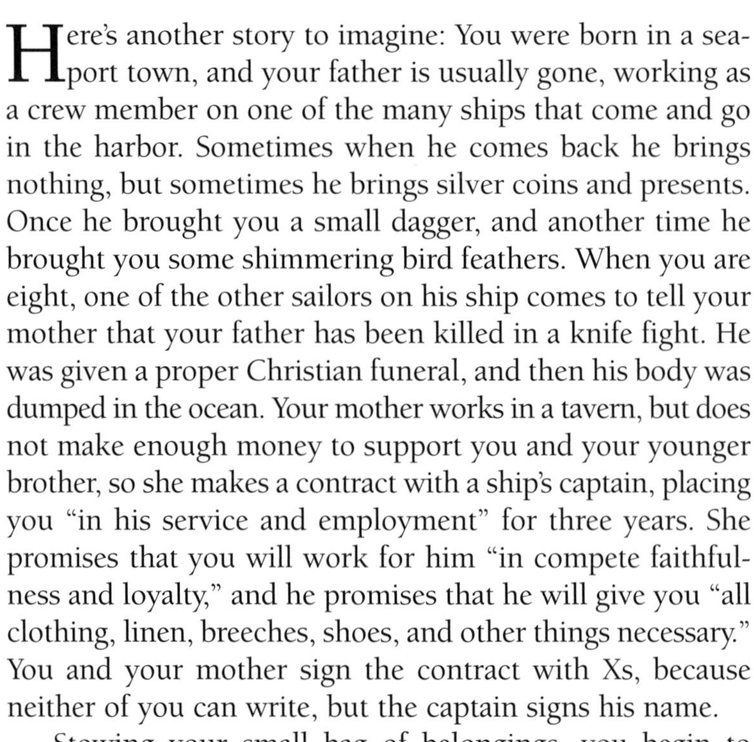

Here's another story to imagine: You were born in a seaport town, and your father is usually gone, working as a crew member on one of the many ships that come and go in the harbor. Sometimes when he comes back he brings nothing, but sometimes he brings silver coins and presents. Once he brought you a small dagger, and another time he brought you some shimmering bird feathers. When you are eight, one of the other sailors on his ship comes to tell your mother that your father has been killed in a knife fight. He was given a proper Christian funeral, and then his body was dumped in the ocean. Your mother works in a tavern, but does not make enough money to support you and your younger brother, so she makes a contract with a ship's captain, placing you "in his service and employment" for three years. She promises that you will work for him "in compete faithfulness and loyalty," and he promises that he will give you "all clothing, linen, breeches, shoes, and other things necessary." You and your mother sign the contract with Xs, because neither of you can write, but the captain signs his name.

Stowing your small bag of belongings, you begin to work with other men and boys to load the ship. On come barrels of wine and water, casks of flour and dried beans, tubs of salted beef and pork. On come guns, gunpowder, and cannon balls. Most of the men and boys are strangers, and they speak different languages, but some of them are

This small wooden sculpture of a Dutch cabin boy blowing a trumpet was carved in Japan. Boys working on ships were such a common sight that nobody paid much attention to them, though ship's captains often began their careers in this lowly position.

people you know from hanging around the docks and taverns. A few of the men are dressed in long black robes, and you know that they are priests. After filling the ship with so many barrels and boxes you can hardly move, and after waiting until the tide and winds are just right, the captain orders the ship to sail. You slowly lose sight of the town, and of your mother, who has run out from the dockside tavern where she works to wave good-bye.

Once you're underway, the winds are sometimes so strong that you worry the ship might tip over, but sometimes they quit blowing, and then the ship stands still. It still moves up and down in the waves, though, so you get very seasick, and spend a lot of time hanging your head over the edge of the deck. It's hot, and much of the water in the barrels has absorbed some salt, so it's not fit to drink. The men on board, and you too, wash down your meals of boiled beans, salt pork, and the hard bread known as ship biscuit with lots of sour wine. The flour has weevils and roaches, which end up in the ship biscuit, though you don't notice this much, because you are so hungry that you eat whatever you are given. You also don't notice the rats that are on the ship very much, although sometimes you and the other boys on board chase them when you aren't working. What you do notice is that as the voyage wears on, your teeth get loose and your gums bleed, so that it gets harder and harder to eat.

The wine, along with the whisky and rum the men get from time to time, make some of the crew rowdy and ready to pick fights. Your father was killed in just such a fight, one of the men on board tells you, although that voyage had been bad all around. One of the ships in the fleet had broken apart on rocks, another had caught fire, some sort of plague had killed much of the crew, and they returned to port with no spices, no gold, and only a few slaves to sell. That captain had been jinxed, the man tells you, but the captain of this ship, whom your mother made the contract with, is much better—a good navigator and experienced

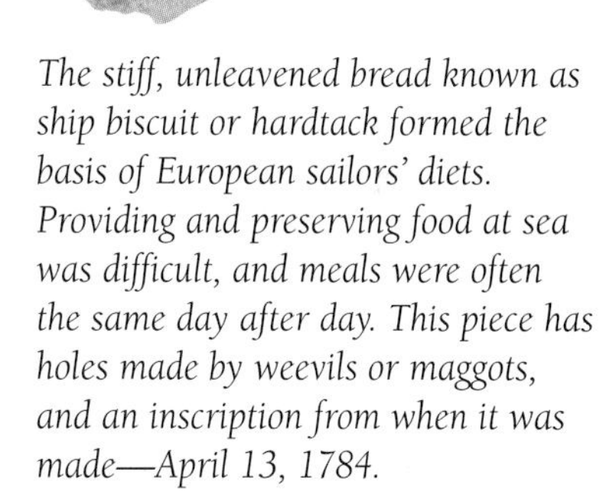

The stiff, unleavened bread known as ship biscuit or hardtack formed the basis of European sailors' diets. Providing and preserving food at sea was difficult, and meals were often the same day after day. This piece has holes made by weevils or maggots, and an inscription from when it was made—April 13, 1784.

sailor who can maintain discipline among the men, even when they are drunk.

You watch the captain and come to agree with your fellow sailor's judgment about his skills, so when your three years are up, you sign on with him again. Over the years, your voyages take you to the west coast of Africa for slaves and gold, to the Indian Ocean for spices and pearls, and to the Americas for silver, sugar, and cochineal insects for making red dye. When you are about 20, you marry a young woman who works as a servant in your hometown. You get back there every two or three years, and send word back to her if you run into others who are going that way sooner. You and she have several children, and the boys also join ships' crews.

This is not the story of a single individual, like Queen Elizabeth, but of experiences shared by many boys and men from the busy port cities of Spain, Portugal, England, and France in the 16th century. Boys like the one in this story would not have learned to read or write, and the captains and conquerors who kept journals and wrote letters glorifying their voyages never tell us the names of their cabin boys.

Flying fish were one of the many new sea creatures that seemed mythical to Europeans who read or heard about them. They could not "fly" over a tall ship as the artist shows them doing in this 1594 engraving, but they could leap out of the water and glide for 100 feet or more, and were— and are— an important source of food in many of the Caribbean islands.

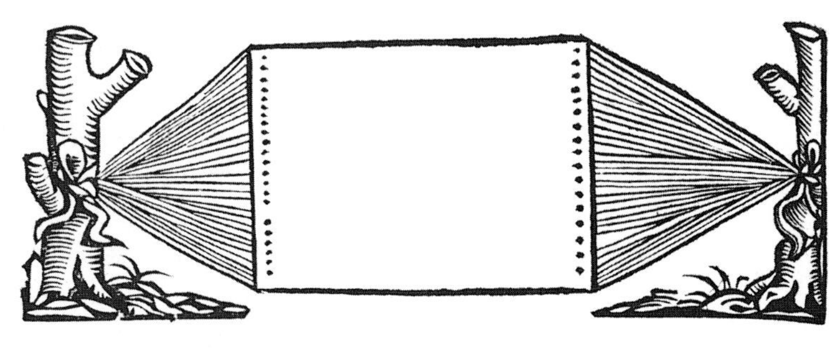

A hammock stretches between two trees, as shown in a history of the West Indies published in Spain in 1535. Columbus discovered hammocks, along with other New World inventions such as the canoe, on his first voyage, and European sailors slowly adopted them to make sleeping on board ship more comfortable.

Those captains recruited crews from the men and boys hanging around the docks hoping to make their fortune, or from among men they knew from earlier trips. They found merchants willing to risk the cash needed to pay for the voyage in hopes of making fabulous profits in return. They scouted around for a few missionaries to go with them, usually monks or priests who were accustomed to a harsh life and so could withstand the rigors of life on a ship.

Voyages were rough and uncomfortable, with no sleeping quarters for anyone except officers, so that the sailors, soldiers, and whoever else was on board slept right on the deck. (In the late 16th century, crews began to use hammocks, the Native American invention that Amerigo Vespucci had described in his letter to the Medicis as "so sweet to sleep in.") Food was monotonous, and the crew was often rough and brutal. Shipwrecks, disease, accidents, malnutrition, and knife fights all killed far more crew members than any battles with an enemy. Many ships and men never returned.

LIKE FISH OUT OF WATER

In the Indian Ocean, Portuguese mariners tried to dominate the centuries-old trade in gold, spices, silk, and other goods. They decided that the best way to do this was to build fortified trading posts along coasts that ships sailed near, or at narrow passageways between bodies of water. They then required all merchant ships sailing by these forts to buy licenses or risk having their cargoes confiscated and their captains executed if they met a Portuguese warship.

Cannons and sturdy ships made this Portuguese racket possible. Indian, Turkish, and Arabic warships were usually long, light rowed galleys that carried just a few cannons, built for quick actions close to shore. Portuguese ships were bulkier and better able to withstand storms at sea. They carried more heavy, long-range guns, able to bombard cities as well as blast holes in other vessels. They often attacked quickly, before galleys were able to travel from their home ports and mount a defense. The Portuguese also threw their opponents off guard with new tactics, such as blockading harbors. The soldiers and sailors on Portuguese ships were the kind of men our imaginary boy encountered: ruthless, rough, and far from home, with no backup plan if they lost.

Sailors climb the rigging while well-dressed merchants gather on deck, in this Japanese painting of Portuguese ships. Portuguese ships were well-armed and fairly safe from pirates, and they carried silver, silk, spices, and other products from one Asian country to another as well as back to Europe.

From their fortified trading posts along the coasts of Africa, India, and Southeast Asia, Portuguese ships landed in China and Japan. Though Chinese emperors did not support long ocean voyages after those of Zheng He, large Chinese cargo ships sailed all over the South China Sea, trading silk and porcelain for pepper, spices, and cotton. They also carried silver mined in Japan back to China, where it was made into coins. This rich trade attracted Portuguese merchants, but when the first of them reached China in the 1520s they were rude to the Chinese, who thought the Portuguese were weak. "They do not know how to fight on land," wrote a Chinese official in a report in 1530, but are "like fishes, which, when you take them out of the water or sea, straightaway die."

In the 1540s, the Chinese officials changed their minds, but not because the Portuguese sailors' manners or fighting ability had improved. Instead, a Japanese ruler allowed the Portuguese to trade in Japan, and bought European guns from the Portuguese to use against his foreign enemies and rival warlords within Japan. The Portuguese sent well-armed large ships to handle this new trade with Japan, and Chinese officials recognized that these ships could also provide safe transport for Japanese silver to China, guarding from capture by pirates or local nobles sailing in the South China Sea. Along with Japanese silver, Portuguese ships also brought American silver and new American crops such as sweet potatoes and corn, which had been brought across the Pacific to the Philippines in Spanish ships. Portuguese merchants grew wealthy by shipping products all over East and Southeast Asia, as well as to Europe and Africa. Portuguese ships also brought Christian missionaries, especially Jesuits, to China. The emperors generally tolerated Christianity because it did not require people to give up their allegiance to the emperor. Christianity joined Confucianism, Taoism, Buddhism, and Islam as a religion practiced in China, though not by very many people.

Though they have a well-equipped army and navy, they are quite content with what they have and are not ambitious of conquest. In this they are much different from the people of Europe, who are frequently discontented with their own governments and envious of what others enjoy.

—Matteo Ricci, a Jesuit missionary who spent nine years at the emperor's court in Beijing, describing the Chinese in his journal, 1600

The Portuguese "empire" in Asia altered trading patterns somewhat, but had little significant impact on the powerful Asian states or on people's daily lives. Except for the small number of converts to Christianity, most people were probably not aware that Europeans had been added to the international mix of merchants and traders that had been active in their coastal cities for thousands of years. If they stayed long enough, in fact, many of those European men married local women and raised children, so they blended even more easily into the multiethnic population. The rulers of Portugal did get some taxes and fees, especially from the silver trade with China, but this money did not make Portugal strong enough to withstand a Spanish invasion and conquest in 1580. The kings of Spain ruled Portugal from 1580 until 1640, which made the flow of silver and other goods back and forth from the Americas to Europe and Asia even smoother.

In the 15th century, the impact of European voyages along the west coast of Africa was not much stronger than in Asia. Tropical diseases such as malaria, yellow fever, and sleeping sickness killed Europeans quickly, so Portuguese traders often stayed only a short while, as close to the coast

A Jesuit priest dressed in Chinese clothing gestures toward a compass, telescope, and other astronomical instruments. European missionaries were welcomed at the Chinese emperor's court, where they discussed religious issues and European advances in astronomy and other areas of science with Confucian scholars.

as possible. They set up permanent fortified trading posts, but relied on existing African trading networks to buy and sell goods. A few missionaries ventured further inland, and in Kongo they had success in gaining converts to Christianity, but this did not alter local life very much.

SUGAR'S BITTER STORY

Sugar changed all this. Sugar may not be physically addictive, but humans love sweetness, and will spend money to add it to their diet. Many plants produce sugar as they grow, but the best producer of sucrose, the kind of sugar we normally eat, is the tall grass plant known as sugarcane. Sugarcane is native to the South Pacific, and was taken to India and China in ancient times. In the Middle Ages, sugar cultivation spread into the Mediterranean, where islands such as Crete, Sicily, and Cyprus had the right kind of warm, wet climate. The Atlantic Islands, off the coast of Africa, also had this kind of climate, and shortly after they were discovered, Portuguese and Italian investors got charters from the Portuguese king to grow and process sugar.

Producing sugar takes both expensive refining machinery and many workers to burn fields so that the cane can be cut more easily, chop and transport heavy cane, and tend vats of cooking cane juice. This means that it is difficult for small growers to produce sugar economically, so large plantations, owned by distant merchants or investors, developed instead. The earliest sugar plantations in Europe and Africa were worked by both free and slave workers from many ethnic groups, but by the 1480s the workers on many sugar plantations, especially those on the Atlantic Islands, were all black African slaves.

Columbus saw sugar production firsthand when he lived on the island of Madeira, and he took sugarcane cuttings to the Caribbean on his second voyage. The first sugar mill in the Western Hemisphere was built in 1515 in what is now the Dominican Republic. Like the Caribbean, Brazil had the right kind of climate for growing sugarcane, and by the middle of the 16th century investors from all over Europe were setting up sugar plantations there as well. By 1600, Brazil was Europe's largest source of sugar, and the sweetener had become a regular part of many people's diets. In England, people were now eating several pounds of sugar each over the course of a year. This amount is still tiny compared to modern sugar consumption (in the United States we eat about 150 pounds a year per person), but much more than it had been in the Middle Ages. At that time, sugar had been such a luxury that people thought of it more as a drug than a food.

Sugar growers in the Caribbean and Brazil first tried to force native peoples to do the backbreaking labor that sugar demands, but they either died or ran away. Few Europeans

Their conversation is so polite that they all seem to have been brought up in the palaces of great nobles. . . . They are very brave and put much faith in their weapons; boys over the age of thirteen carry a sword and a dagger.

—Jesuit missionary Cosme de Torres, comments on the Japanese in a report to his superiors, 1550s

The Sole Trade in This Island

RICHARD LIGON, TRUE AND EXACT HISTORY OF THE ISLAND OF BARBADOES, 1673

Richard Ligon was an English sugar planter on the Caribbean island of Barbados, just when this island was becoming the main supplier of sugar for Britain. He included a long discussion of sugar growing and processing, and the slave system that supported it, in the history of Barbados that he wrote in 1673, late in his life. In his book, Ligon uses the word "Christian" to refer to Europeans, though some of the African slaves were also Christian.

The work of sugar making... is now grown the sole trade in this island.... It has been accounted a strange thing, that the Negroes, being more than double the number of Christians that there are, and they accounted a bloody people... should not commit some horrible massacre upon the Christians thereby to enfranchise [free] themselves and become masters of the island. But there are three reasons that they do not: the one is, that they are not suffered [allowed] to touch or handle any weapons, the other, that they are held in such awe [fear] and slavery as they are fearful to appear in any daring act... the third reason... is that they are fetched from several parts of Africa who speak several languages. And by that means one of them understands not another....

[After giving birth], in a fortnight [two weeks] this woman is at work with her child at her back, as merry a soul as any there is. If the overseer be discreet [has good judgment], she is suffered to rest herself a little more than ordinary; but if not, she is compelled to do as others do. Times they have of suckling their children in the fields, and refreshing themselves; and good reason, for they carry their burdens on their backs, and yet work too.... The work which women do is most of it weeding, a stooping and painful work.

Pieces of bronze hardware for sailing vessels from the 16th century were also used to buy slaves on the West African coast. The large one was the price of an adult, and the smaller ones would buy children.

were willing to wield machetes and haul cane in the hot sun for any amount of wages. So planters did what had been done on the Atlantic Islands—they imported enslaved Africans to work on the huge plantations they set up. The slave traders in West Africa adopted more aggressive tactics to meet this new demand for laborers. "Notwithstanding the sickness of our men," wrote Sir John Hawkins, an English sea captain and slave trader, in a report in 1568, "we assaulted the town both by land and sea, and very fiercely with fire (their houses being covered with dry palm leaves) captured the town, and put the inhabitants to flight. We took 250 persons, men, women, and children."

Slaves work on a sugar plantation on the Caribbean island of Hispaniola, now Haiti and the Dominican Republic. This 1595 engraving shows men with different skin tones, but most slaves by this point were of African ancestry, though some may have been Native American or of mixed race.

The slave trade grew steadily, and first thousands and then tens of thousands of people a year were taken from Africa to work on sugar plantations. Slaves were marched from the interior of Africa to the coast, where they waited in locked pens to be loaded onto ships. They were crowded into the filthy, stinking space below the ships' decks, sometimes with not enough room to sit up. Food and water were limited for everyone on board, and even more so for slaves, who also suffered beatings and brutal treatment at the hands of the crew. Early on in the slave trade, as many as half the captives died on the trip across the Atlantic—called the "middle passage"—though later the death rate declined as ship owners realized that they could make better profits if they kept the slaves alive. At every stage, slaves resisted their capture by refusing to work, sabotaging equipment, running away, or rebelling. In most islands of the Caribbean and on the South American mainland, communities of escaped slaves, known as "maroons," came together in forested or swampy areas, free from the control of plantation owners or government officials.

> *Concerning buying and selling, they are all brought together in a large plain, where, by our surgeons, they are thoroughly examined, and that naked both men and women.... Those which are approved as good are set to one side; in the meanwhile a burning iron, with the name of the company, lies in the fire, with which ours are marked on the breast.*
>
> —Willem Bosman, a Dutch slave trader, describes a slave station on the west coast of Africa in *New and Accurate Description of the Coast of Guinea*, 1705

Slavery was a part of many societies around the world in 1500, but the plantation slavery of the New World was different from earlier slavery in two ways. First, almost all the slaves were black, and almost all the owners and managers were white. Plantation slavery had a racial element that slavery in other parts of the world did not. Both European Christians and Arabic Muslims saw black Africans as inferior, barbaric, and primitive. Such attitudes allowed people to buy and sell African slaves without any moral concerns, and the plantation system strengthened these racist ideas.

Plantation owners came to think of their slaves more as machines than as people. Like machines, slaves would wear out and need replacing. Brazilian owners figured that most slaves would live about seven years, and they calculated the costs of buying new slaves into the price they hoped to get for their sugar. Slaves were not treated exactly like machines, however. A plantation owner would never think of punishing a machine, but, because they were considered responsible for their own actions, slaves could be punished for mistakes or any behavior the owners did not like. But they were property, and the children of slave women were property, too. Our imaginary European cabin boy had a difficult life, but African children captured and transported as slaves, or born as slaves in the Americas, had lives that were still more brutal. Some Christian missionaries objected

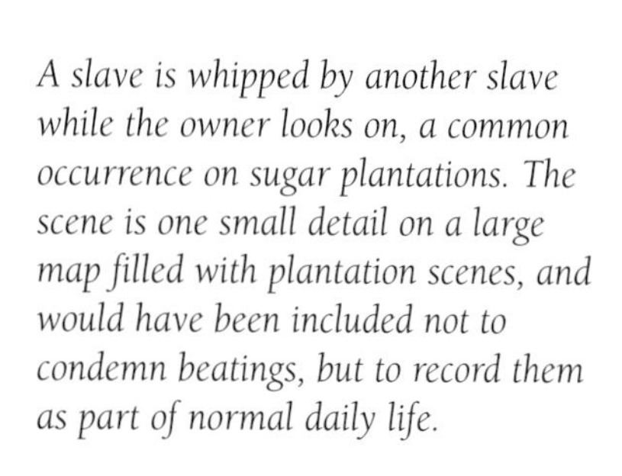

A slave is whipped by another slave while the owner looks on, a common occurrence on sugar plantations. The scene is one small detail on a large map filled with plantation scenes, and would have been included not to condemn beatings, but to record them as part of normal daily life.

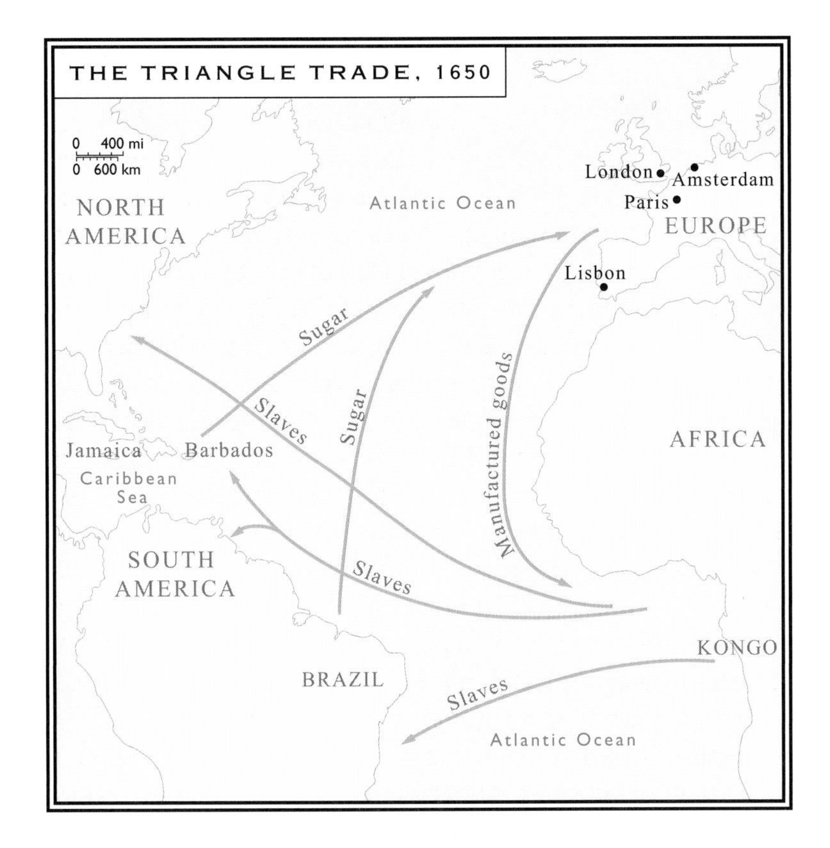

In this map, the arrows indicating the triangle-trade routes do not touch specific points on land because each corner of the triangle actually consisted of many ports. For example, slave ships left from at least six or seven places along the west coast of Africa, and would land in ports throughout the Americas and the Caribbean islands.

to the treatment of slaves, especially if the slaves had converted to Christianity, but the Catholic and Protestant churches did not directly oppose slavery.

The second new thing about plantation slavery was how much it depended on the international trade. Each plantation only grew one thing: at first, most grew sugar, and later others cultivated crops such as coffee, indigo, and cotton. That meant that everything else needed on the plantation had to be brought in—food, clothing, and tools. Ships that brought slaves from Africa to the Caribbean and Brazil (and later, in smaller numbers, to North America and the rest of South America) took sugar and molasses from the Americas to Europe, and brought European cloth and manufactured goods to Africa and the Caribbean. Or they took flour and lumber from North America to tropical plantations, and carried molasses on the way back to North America, where it was processed into rum.

Slaves were held at these two forts on the West African coast while waiting to be loaded onto ships bound for the Caribbean and other parts of the New World. The smaller boats and rafts ferried trade goods and slaves back and forth between land and the ships anchored in deep water offshore.

In Europe, the sugar was used to make sweet wine in Portugal or the Atlantic Islands, which was shipped to England in exchange for cloth and machines. One kind of sweet wine is still called Madeira, the name of the island where Columbus and his family had lived. Rum and wine were on every European ship crossing any ocean, for they could be sold at a profit almost anywhere and were part of the crews' daily rations. West Africa, Europe, and the Caribbean formed three points in what is often called the "triangle trade" of the Atlantic, and any leg of this triangle offered opportunities for wealth.

Slavery may seem like a very backward way of doing things, but in some ways plantations were like efficient modern factories, mass producing one specific item to be sold as widely as possible. The slave trade by itself did not bring spectacular profits, but the plantations it made possible were an essential part of a business network that provided steadily increasing wealth for European merchants and investors. During the 16th century, European governments expanded their navies to help control pirates and built more and better seaports, making trade a bit more secure. In the century after Columbus's journey, captains and investors knew they were still taking risks with ocean voyages, but the possibilities of profit usually outweighed those risks. The number of ships sailing out from European ports increased steadily, and boys could always find a job on them.

CHAPTER 12

GERMS, SILVER, AND BLOOD

NEW WORLD CONQUESTS AND GLOBAL CONNECTIONS

Broken spears lie in the roads;
we have torn our hair in grief . . .
for our inheritance, our city, is lost and dead.
The shields of our warriors were its defense, but they could not save it.

So wrote an Aztec whose name we don't know, describing the conquest of his land in central Mexico by troops under the leadership of Hernán Cortés, an ambitious Spanish nobleman who had come to the West Indies when he was still a teenager. For 25 years after Columbus's first voyage, Spanish settlements in the New World were limited to islands in the Caribbean, though explorers went back and forth to the American mainland several times. Spanish horses and Spanish soldiers gradually grew more accustomed to tropical climates, and in 1519 Cortés led a group of six hundred men, several hundred horses, and many dogs to the east coast of Mexico, looking for gold.

This drawing by an Aztec artist, preserved in an illustrated history of the Aztecs written by a Spanish priest in the late 16th century, shows the Aztec emperor distributing food and clothing to his people. He appears benevolent, but these goods had often been taken from conquered peoples, making them resent the Aztecs.

Mexico was ruled by the Aztecs, a group of people who had migrated into central Mexico from the north beginning about 1300, and conquered the people already living there. Their capital was at Tenochtitlan, built on islands in Lake Texcoco in the central valley of Mexico.

As the [Aztec] people had developed as daring and warlike, they gave vent to their spirit by overcoming their neighbors. . . . He [Moctezuma] demanded that they pay much in tribute . . . and since they were so feared, no one dared countermand [go against] or overstep his will and order.

—An Aztec chronicler describing the conquest of neighboring tribes before the Spanish arrived, from a history of the Aztec Empire handwritten in Spanish in 1539, 20 years after Cortés's conquest

Aztec warriors gained prestige and land through their conquests, and the Aztecs came to see war as a religious duty. They believed that the all-important sun god demanded the sacrifice of captured enemy warriors and other youthful victims to maintain his energy so that crops would grow and life could continue. Because of this, Aztec warriors took prisoners instead of killing defeated soldiers on the battlefield. They also demanded that conquered tribes pay tribute and supply additional people for ritual sacrifice. By the time Spanish troops reached Mexico, the Aztec Empire contained many groups of people who hated the Aztecs.

With the help of a Spanish soldier who spoke one Native American language, and a local woman who spoke several, Cortés gathered allies from the enemies of the Aztecs. Those who were unwilling to side with him at first often changed their minds when he used cannons to bombard their villages. The Aztec Emperor Moctezuma II sent messengers to see what Cortés wanted. "All iron was their war array," reported a messenger to Moctezuma in 1519, and their "very large" dogs had "fiery yellow eyes." When they fired their guns and cannons "it thundered" and "fire went showering forth." Whatever the cannons hit, the messenger told the emperor, was "destroyed, dissolved, vanished." By the time he reached Tenochtitlan, Cortés had several thousand troops.

Aztec tradition required hospitality to visitors, and Emperor Moctezuma let Cortés and his followers into the city. They repaid this welcome by fighting their hosts, and capturing and killing the emperor. The Aztecs threw the Spaniards out of the city in a bloody battle. Cortés gained more allies from among the Aztecs' enemies, and after a long siege took Tenochtilan. He and his allies then fought Aztec armies in other areas, and by 1521 Cortés took permanent control of the whole empire. He shipped Aztec art back to Europe, where it was seen and appreciated by Renaissance artists. The German artist Albrecht Dürer saw an exhibit of Aztec art, and wrote in his diary in 1520, "All the days of my life I have seen nothing that rejoiced my heart so much as these things, for I have seen among them

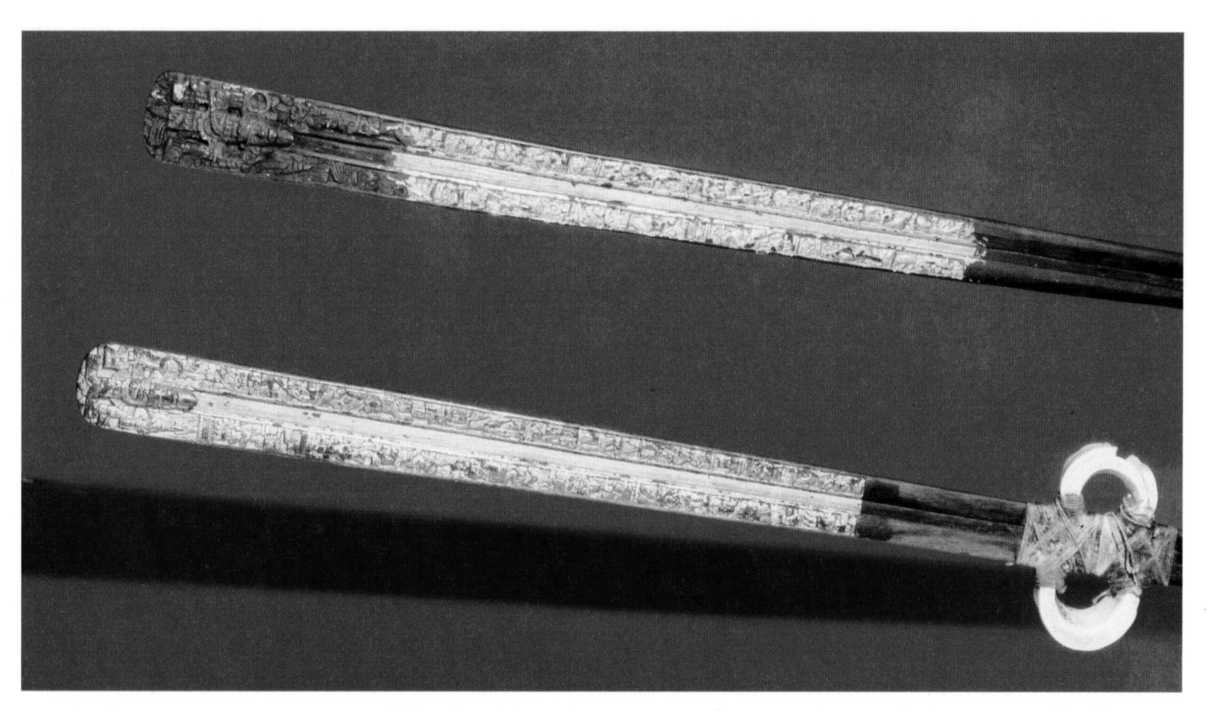

wonderful works of art, and I marveled at the subtle intellect of men in foreign parts."

Local allies and weapons that used gunpowder are two important reasons why Cortés was able to defeat an empire of about 20 million people with a tiny force. The main reason was much smaller, however—germs. The impact of European voyages was devastating, even for people who never saw a ship or a soldier. Europeans brought with them diseases that were common in Eurasia, such as measles, mumps, bubonic plague, influenza, and smallpox, against which natives of the Americas had no resistance.

These diseases spread through the Caribbean Islands, and then to the mainland of the Americas. When Cortés and his followers entered Tenochtitlan, they carried smallpox germs, against which even the best military defenses were helpless. This invisible enemy killed thousands of people, and the weakened Aztec forces could not withstand later attacks, even though Cortés's local allies were also dying at a fast pace.

continues on page 170

Atlatls, or spear-throwers, allowed Aztec warriors to throw spears much farther than they could using just their arms. Spears fit into the groove between the carved scenes of gods and battles on these two gilded atlatls.

A Great Many Died

AN AZTEC ACCOUNT OF CORTÉS'S CONQUEST OF MEXICO, 1528

Several Aztec chronicles describe Cortés's conquest of the Aztec Empire. Emperor Moctezuma II received reports of his progress from the coast. When Cortés got to Tenochtitlan, Moctezuma greeted him as he did any visiting lord, giving him gifts and offering his hospitality. People later said that the Aztecs were amazed by Cortés and thought he was a god, but Aztec reports from the time do not say this. They do talk a great deal about the Europeans' weapons, horses, and iron armor. They also discuss the importance of other tribes who allied themselves with the Spaniards, and the devastating effects of disease. The author of this anonymous account, written in the language of the Aztecs, was an eyewitness to the events.

Moctezuma went out to meet them. He presented many gifts to the Captain [Cortés] and his commanders, those who had come to make war. He showered gifts upon them and hung flowers around their necks.... Then he hung the gold necklaces around their necks and gave them presents of every sort as gifts of welcome....

The envoys [from Moctezuma] made sacrifices in front of the Captain. At this, he grew very angry. When they offered him blood in an "eagle dish," he shouted at the man who offered it and struck him with his sword. The envoys departed at once.

Then the Captain marched to Tenochtitlan.... When the Spaniards entered the Royal House, they placed Moctezuma under guard and kept him under their vigilance.... Then the Spaniards fired one of their cannons, and this caused great confusion in the city. The people scattered in every direction.... In the morning the Spaniards told Moctezuma what they needed in the way of supplies: tortillas, fried chickens, hens' eggs, pure water, firewood, and charcoal.... Moctezuma ordered that it be sent to them....

During this time, the people asked Moctezuma how they should celebrate their god's fiesta. He said, "Dress him in all his finery, in all his sacred ornaments."...

When this had been done, the celebrants began to sing their songs... but without warning they were put to death. The dancers and singers were completely unarmed. . . . The Spaniards attacked the musicians first, slashing at their hands and faces until they had killed all of them. The singers—and even the spectators—were also killed. This slaughter in the Sacred Patio went on for three hours. Then the Spaniards burst into the rooms of the temple to kill the others: those who were carrying water, or bringing fodder for the horses. Or grinding meal, or sweeping, or standing watch over this work. . . .

They [the Spaniards] all ran forward, armed as if for battle. . . . They attacked all the celebrants, stabbing them, spearing them, striking them from behind, and these fell instantly to the ground with their entrails hanging out. . . . They began to shoot at the Mexicans with their iron arrows and to fire their cannons and arquebuses [an early form of firearm]. . . . A vast number of our warriors were killed by their metal darts. . . . The women joined in the fighting. They struck at the enemy and shot arrows at them; they tucked up their skirts and dressed in the regalia of war. . . .

[Later] a great plague broke out here in Tenochtitlan. It began to spread during the thirteenth month and lasted for seventy days, striking everywhere in the city and killing a vast number of our people. Sores erupted on our faces, our breasts, our bellies; we were covered with agonizing sores from head to foot.

The illness was so dreadful that no one could walk or move. . . . A great many died from the plague, and many others died of hunger. They could not get up to search for food, and everyone else was too sick to care for them, so they starved to death in their beds.

Cortés and his armored troops march across Mexico, with native people carrying supplies on their backs. The bearded Cortés is accompanied by his African servant and the native woman who served as his translator.

continued from page 167

Disease often attacked local populations before the soldiers arrived. For germs to be transmitted, only a few or even one native person had to come into contact with a Spanish landing party and then return to their village. Germs spread to other people as they did normal things such as preparing food, carrying children, or talking about

THE AZTEC AND INCA EMPIRES, 1500

what they had seen. People became sick and died quickly, so that when Spanish troops got to an area several weeks or months later, they found people who were already weak and fewer in number. Demographers, people who study the rise and fall of population, estimate that within several decades after the Spanish conquest about 90 percent of the population of Central America died, and similar numbers in some parts of South America.

AN EMPIRE IN THE MOUNTAINS WITH A SILVER LINING

Guns and germs were also both important in the Spanish conquest of the largest empire in South America, that of the Incas in the Andes Mountains. Like the Aztecs, the Incas built their empire through military conquest, which by 1520 stretched for three thousand miles along the west coast of South America. They demanded tribute and taxes in the form of crops and forced labor from the people they conquered. One of the most important tasks throughout the Inca Empire was building and maintaining roads and bridges. Roads made it easier to transport food and for messengers and armies to move swiftly. Along the roads, the Incas built special huts for runners, who carried oral messages to the runner in the next hut, a sort of pony express by mouth and on foot. This system allowed news to travel about 150 miles a day, but it would also allow infectious diseases to be carried just as swiftly.

A runner travels one of the many Inca roads, carrying the knotted strings called quipu that recorded messages, and blowing on a shell trumpet to let people know he is coming. Made in the late 16th century, this drawing is one of many sent to the Spanish king along with a history of the Inca Empire written by an Inca nobleman.

In 1525, the powerful Inca emperor died of an epidemic disease that also killed many other people. We don't know if this disease was smallpox brought by the Spanish, but it might have been, as smallpox had already spread into the Andes from Central America. There were disagreements among the Incas about who should be the next emperor. At the same time, Francisco Pizarro, a Spanish adventurer who had become rich after settling in Panama City, heard stories of a fabulous Indian empire somewhere to the south. Pizarro was the son of a soldier and had so little education that he never learned to read, but he was an effective leader of men like himself. He organized several expeditions to search for the Andean empire, gaining allies from among groups who resented the Incas' power.

In 1533, Pizarro reached the Inca capital of Cuzco, called the Inca ruling elites together for a meeting in the city's main square, and killed most of them. The leader who many Incas backed as the next emperor, Atahualpa, paid a huge ransom in gold and silver for his release, but the Spaniards strangled him anyway, and then cut off his head. With no leader, and disease spreading through the population, the Inca Empire fell to the Spanish, and Pizarro founded the city of Lima as the capital of this new colony. The Spanish used Lima as a base for the exploration and conquest of most of South America. King Charles I of Spain made Pizarro governor of Peru, as the Spaniards named their new colony in South America, but he was killed a few years later by another Spanish explorer who wanted to be governor.

Atahualpa was the last Inca emperor. This portrait, painted after the Spanish conquest by an unknown artist, shows him in elaborate clothing decorated with gold and feathers, not much different from that worn by European royalty such as King Henry VIII of England, who lived at exactly the same time.

King Charles of Spain—the same King Charles who became the German emperor, listened to Luther, and sent Magellan around the world—also made Cortés governor of Mexico, which was renamed New Spain. In both Central and South America, the Spaniards founded new towns, built Christian churches, and set up agricultural plantations like those in the Caribbean. Spanish missionaries began preaching to the local residents, first in Spanish, which few people understood. Later, some missionaries learned the languages spoken in the Americas. They set up missions away from the new Spanish towns and from existing Indian villages, and tried to convert native people to Christianity and to teach them European ways. The missions took the local people away from their own culture, but also protected them from plantation owners who wanted to enslave them.

Spanish troops with horses, cannons, and firearms attack the Incas and arrest Atahualpa. Atahualpa had his people fill a room with gold and silver to pay his ransom, but Pizarro ordered him killed anyway.

When the Spanish discovered silver mines in northern Mexico and in the Andes Mountains of Peru, they sent more soldiers to conquer territory faster. Silver was very important to the European economy. Though merchants and bankers in Europe and Asia occasionally used paper money for very large business transactions, most buying and selling was done with coins. And most of these coins were silver, which people also used to pay their taxes. More silver meant more coins available, and also more revenue for the government, which taxed both mining and trade.

The Spanish government saw the silver mines as a great opportunity, and granted the rights to mine silver to private investors in exchange for 20 percent of the silver they mined. Mine owners brought in managers with experience mining in Europe, installed machinery and materials to smelt the silver ore and make it pure, and imported goods so they could live as wealthy people did in Europe. The Spanish government wanted to make sure this silver got back to Europe, so they built forts, encouraged the construction of sturdier ships and better weapons, and hired troops. In the Andes, they adapted the system of forced labor the Incas had used to build their empire, compelling Indians to mine and transport silver from the unbelievably rich mines at Potosí.

The Indians were also forced to mine mercury, which was needed to extract the silver from silver ore but is also highly poisonous. Mission priests sometimes objected to the Spaniards' cruel treatment of the Indians. One priest who had spent many years in the Americas wrote in a letter to the Spanish king in 1541 that the Indians, "drop from hunger and thirst as they stumble through the mountains with enormous loads on their backs, and the Spanish kick them and beat them with sticks." "More than 3,000 Indians work away hard with picks and hammers," wrote another in a 1625 history titled *Compendium and Description of the West Indies,* "and when they have filled their sacks, the poor fellows, loaded with ore, climb up those ladders or rigging, some like masts and others like cables, and so trying and distressing that a man empty-handed can hardly get up them." The government often replaced priests who protested with others more willing to follow orders.

Residents of the Andes pan for metal in mountain streams in an illustration from a French manuscript. Before the Spanish conquest, silver and gold were obtained in South America primarily from the earth's surface or from shallow mines. The Spanish brought in German engineers who were experienced in deep tunnel mining.

The Spanish government could do nothing about the spread of germs, however. Dangerous conditions in the mines and poisoning from the mercury combined with disease to kill people at alarming rates. Especially in the Andes, people fled to remote villages rather than work in mines, and there weren't enough Spanish troops to force the workers to return. The Spaniards brought in some African slaves from their Caribbean colonies, because they would not have local family connections and so would find it harder to run away, but they also died in great numbers. The mine owners responded to problems in finding and keeping workers by trying new types of more efficient machinery, and eventually by providing wages and improving working conditions. The forced labor of native people survived in some areas until the 18th century, however, and the enslavement of Africans even longer.

Spanish officials had originally imagined that their colonies in Central and South America would contain separate communities of Europeans and Indians. A hundred years after conquest this was partly true. In the early 1600s, there were perhaps 200,000 people in the Spanish colonies who were, or pretended to be, of purely European ancestry. They lived in cities, wore clothing made of English wool or Chinese silk, ate off Dutch dishes, drank sweet Portuguese wine, and worshiped in churches designed by Italian architects. This European minority held the positions of power in the government, church, and private business. Away from the cities, there were millions of people of purely Indian ancestry living in villages, hunting or raising the same animals and growing the same crops they had for centuries. This was especially true in areas such as the Amazon River basin where there were no precious metals and no possibility of growing sugar. European diseases had killed people even in the most remote areas, but Spanish officials or soldiers rarely traveled in these areas, and very few missionaries ventured there.

The number of European women who migrated to the Spanish and Portuguese colonies was much smaller than the number of men, however, so the Europeans could not continue to live apart from the Native Americans and Africans. European men entered into relationships with native or slave women, and a mixed, or mestizo, society developed, especially in and around mining towns and the new cities. The children of mestizos married Indians, Africans, Europeans, or other mestizos, increasing the number and variety of people with mixed parentage.

As time went on, the number of mestizos grew, especially in Mexico and Brazil, where they came to outnumber

Your majesty must be aware that the mine-owners who dress up in silk and brocade are spending a great deal of money. The only way they can get it is by ill-treating their workers, who are not only overworked, but whipped like children . . . even the chiefs are tortured by being suspended by their feet.

—Guamán Poma, a Peruvian official, describes the mines in Peru in an 800-page letter to King Charles of Spain, written between 1580 and 1615

A wealthy Mexican couple dressed themselves in fancy clothing for their portrait, and their child holds a banana, a fruit first grown in the New World by Portuguese who had learned to grow them from Africans. By the end of the 16th century, much of the population of Mexico, especially in the cities, was mestizo, or of mixed European, Native American, and African heritage.

the people of purely native or purely European ancestry. Most mestizos were Christians, and their church services, buildings, decorations, hymns, and holidays combined European, Indian, and African traditions. This blended heritage was also found in other aspects of culture, such as music and food.

Europeans regarded themselves as superior to the people they had conquered or enslaved, and thought that mestizo people with more European ancestry (what they often called having "Spanish" or "Portuguese" blood) were superior to those with less. Government and church officials in Latin America set up a complicated hierarchy of mixed-background categories, inventing names for many different types of mixtures. Ideas about what we now call race grew out of this hierarchy based on ancestry and "blood." There were no birth certificates, however, so it was very hard to prove someone's ancestry, and most people judged this by the way people looked. Lighter-skinned mixed-background people were given a higher rank than darker-skinned people. People recognized, as we do today, that skin tone and physical features can be very different among close relatives or even brothers and sisters, but the idea that "white" was superior to "black" became so powerful that people ignored what they knew.

FROM TRADE TRIANGLE TO WORLD WIDE WEB

In a few generations, Latin American society had been altered dramatically. Silver mining was an important cause of this rapid change, and silver was also behind the trading partnerships that quickly developed around the world. Silver from Mexico and Peru went to Spain, and beginning in the 1560s several huge ships carrying silver also sailed every year from Acapulco in Mexico to Manila in the Spanish colony of the Philippines. There the silver was traded to Chinese merchants for silk, porcelain, spices, and other luxury goods, to be sold to European mine owners and city dwellers in Latin America or carried still farther to wealthy people in Spain. Those Chinese merchants also bought Japanese silver, and took it all to China, where the expanding economy required more and more silver to make coins. Silver taken to Spain paid for equipment and supplies for both mines and sugar plantations in the colonies, and also for guns and tools taken to West Africa, where they were traded for slaves.

Silver linked the "triangle trade" of the Atlantic Ocean with the networks of spices and silk in the Indian Ocean and the South China Sea. By the early 1600s, European investors could gain a profit from every leg of this trade much more securely than they had been able to a century earlier. The riches of the silver mines had led other Spanish explorers to search for cities of gold in what are now Argentina, Paraguay, Colombia, Venezuela, and the states of Florida, Arizona, and New Mexico. They never found as much gold as they hoped, but merchants and investors had found a source of wealth in trade that was just as valuable as gold, if not quite as exciting.

Gold and silver were useful as metal for coins, but they were also beautiful, and the art that developed in Europe after 1600, called baroque, used lots of gold and silver. Trading ships also carried other products that brought pleasure. We have already seen how sugarcane was brought from Asia to the Americas. Chocolate, which the Aztecs believed had been brought from paradise, went in the other direction. Both the Aztecs and the Mayas cultivated the cacao beans from which chocolate is made, and Cortés took them to Spain. Like the Aztecs, the Spanish developed the habit of

Inca artisans crafted this toucan of hammered gold and turquoise. The rulers of the Inca Empire grew wealthy from taxes and tribute, and they surrounded themselves with beautiful things.

A fashionable French couple drinks hot chocolate. An African servant—or slave—brings ingredients on a tray, while a European servant or friend twirls a whisk in a pot to make the hot chocolate foamy, just as Mexicans still do today with a wooden whisk called a molinillo.

drinking cups of chocolate, which they sweetened with imported sugar. (Aztecs and Mayas drank their chocolate, a word that comes from the Maya words for "sour water," unsweetened.) Drinking chocolate spread to France and England, where by the 1600s people were also drinking coffee imported from Arabia and Africa, and by the 1650s tea imported from India and China. (Coffee-growing in the Americas came later.)

By the 1600s global trade was providing another addictive substance along with the caffeine found in chocolate, tea, and coffee—nicotine, the active chemical in tobacco. Native Americans grew and smoked tobacco long before the arrival of Columbus, who took some tobacco seeds back to Spain with him. Farmers began to grow tobacco for use as what they thought of as a medicine to help people relax. A French diplomat named Jean Nicot—whose name is the origin of the botanical name for tobacco, *Nicotiana,* and of the word "nicotine"—introduced the use of tobacco in France. English merchants brought tobacco to the Ottoman Empire, where coffeehouses filled with pipe smoke became popular places for men to gather. Ottoman religious leaders complained that coffeehouses kept people away from their religious duties, and one sultan tried to outlaw both coffee and tobacco, but he was not very successful.

Global connections were not just a matter of trade, however. The voyages of Columbus and other explorers linked parts of the world that had been cut off from each other for thousands of years. These links were sometimes disastrous, like the spread of infectious diseases to which the people in the Americas had no immunity. But others of these links, what historians call the Columbian Exchange, were very beneficial. Food crops and animals traveled both ways across the Atlantic.

Europeans brought horses, cattle, pigs, sheep, and chickens from Europe, and they also brought wheat, which grew well on the plains of both North America and South America. They took corn and potatoes back to Europe, growing them first as food for animals and gradually as food for people as well. Tomatoes, peppers, sweet potatoes, and peanuts went from South America to Africa and Asia, as did pineapples and avocados. This Columbian Exchange of plants and animals improved nutrition around the world, and allowed a slow increase in the total global population, despite the tremendous loss of life because of infectious disease.

Men and women in many parts of the globe lived in a world that was far more interconnected in 1600 than it had been in 1350. People of great power and those of more limited means came to live their lives differently because of this expanding web of shared knowledge and trade.

The altars of the Jesuit Church in Lima [Peru] are made of finely worked and thick silver. The altar curtains are all of crimson velvet, all adorned on top with solid silver and so high they reach the church's ceiling. They have infinite riches in this monastery.

—Pedro de León Portocarrero, a converted Jew who went to Peru to escape the Spanish Inquisition, describes Lima in a letter, 1600

GLOSSARY

apprentice Someone starting to learn a trade by working for a master in that trade

bestiary Book describing animals, both real and imaginary

block-book Printed book made by carving entire pages in blocks of wood and stamping the inked blocks onto paper

buboes Swellings in the neck, groin, and armpits that are symptoms of bubonic plague

caravel Ship carrying several different types of sails in order to be able to use winds from different directions; some of Columbus's ships were caravels

cochineal insects Small insects that live on cactus in the Americas and are used to make an edible red dye used in foods and for cloth

Confucian ideas Ideas about the best way to live, developed by the Chinese thinker Confucius, which emphasize hierarchy in society, respect for elders and for authority, public service, and education

diplomacy Art of negotiating with other countries to settle disputes without using force

dynasty Succession of rulers from the same family line or group

flagellants People who beat themselves to repent for the sins that they believed caused the plague

gunpowder empire Empire that maintained its power through the use of guns and cannons

heretic One who believes a heresy, or false doctrine

hierarchy Structure in which groups are arranged in a particular order, each more powerful or important than the one below it

humanism Approach to education started in Europe during the Renaissance, focused on classical ancient Latin and Greek writings

inquisition Religious trial used to enforce Christian beliefs

Janissaries Elite soldiers serving Ottoman sultans

journeyman Someone with more experience in a trade than an apprentice, but still not as much experience as a master of the trade

manikongo Ruler of Kongo

maroons Fugitive slaves in the West Indies who created communities hidden from plantation owners and government officials

mestizo Person of mixed Native American, European, and/or African ancestry

neo-Confucianism Revival of Confucius's ideas in the 16th century

printer's devil Printer's apprentice; also an imaginary spirit that would cause printing errors

Protestant Reformation Movement started in the 1500s to reform the Catholic Church

Renaissance Age of artistic and cultural rebirth in Europe, 1300s–1600s

sakk Arabic word for a letter of credit stating that the bearer had money deposited elsewhere

scholar-official Person educated in Confucian ideas and holding a high position in Chinese government

ship biscuit Stiff, unleavened bread, also known as hardtack, that formed the basis of European sailors' diets

triangle trade Network of trade created by the movement of slaves from Africa to the Americas to cultivate sugarcane, sugar from the Americas to Europe, and manufactured goods from Europe to Africa, where they were traded for slaves

tribute Payments (often in the form of goods and labor) that rulers demanded from their subjects

type Separate stamps for printing each letter of the alphabet, also called "movable type" because the pieces of type can be rearranged to form different words

virtù Niccolò Machiavelli's term for the ability of effective rulers to shape the world around them

vizier High executive officer of the Ottoman Empire

warlord Military ruler of a fairly small area

TIMELINE

1337–1453
Hundred Years' War in Europe

1338
Plague spreads in Near East, Europe, and North Africa

1350s
Petrarch begins to teach in Florence

1368
Ming dynasty founded in China

1380s–1405
Tamerlane rules in Central and South Asia

1405–1433
Zheng He travels in Indian Ocean

1441
First African slaves shipped to Portugal

1450s
Gutenberg invents printing press

1492
Columbus's first voyage, Kingdom of Granada falls, Jews expelled from Spain

1493–1528
Askia the Great rules Songhay Empire

1494
Treaty of Tordesillas divides the world between Spain and Portugal

1497
John Cabot leads first English voyage to North America

1498
Vasco da Gama reaches India

1502
First African slaves arrive in Americas

1503
Leonardo da Vinci paints *Mona Lisa*

1506–1543
King Afonso I rules Kongo

1510s
Guru Nanak Devi Ji begins teaching

1513
Machiavelli writes *The Prince*

1515
First sugar mill built in Western Hemisphere

1519–1521
Magellan leads voyage around the world

1520s
Protestant Reformation begins

1521
Hernán Cortés conquers Aztec Empire

1520–1566
Suleyman the Magnificent rules Ottoman Empire

1533
Francisco Pizarro conquers Inca Empire

1540
Ignatius Loyola establishes the Jesuits

1540s
Silver discovered in Peru

1555–1603
Queen Elizabeth I rules England

1556–1605
Akbar the Great rules India

1556–1598
King Philip II rules Spain

1588
Spanish Armada launched and defeated

FURTHER READING

Entries with [“] indicate primary source material.

GENERAL WORKS

Bauer, Susan Wise. *The Story of the World: History for the Classical Child.* Vol. 3, *Early Modern Times.* Richmond, Va.: Peace Hill, 2004.

Brewer, Paul. *Warfare in the Renaissance World.* Austin, Tex.: Raintree Steck-Vaughn, 1999.

ANTHOLOGIES OF PRIMARY SOURCES

[“] Chojnacka, Monica, and Merry Wiesner-Hanks, eds. *Ages of Woman, Ages of Man: Sources in European Social History 1400–1750.* London: Longman, 2002.

[“] Ross, James Bruce, and Mary Martin McLaughlin, eds. *The Portable Renaissance Reader.* New York: Penguin, 1978.

ATLASES

Haywood, John. *World Atlas of the Past, vol. 2: The Medieval World, AD 1 to 1492.* New York: Oxford University Press, 1999.

———. *World Atlas of the Past, vol. 3: The Age of Discovery, 1492 to 1815.* New York: Oxford University Press, 1999.

BIOGRAPHY

Burch, Joann Johansen, and Kent Alan Aldrich. *Fine Print: A Story about Johann Gutenberg.* Minneapolis: Carolrhoda, 1992.

[“] Columbus, Christopher. *I, Columbus: My Journal, 1492–3.* Edited by Peter and Connie Roop. New York: Walker, 1990.

Havelin, Kate. *Queen Elizabeth I.* Minneapolis: Lerner, 2002. 112 pp

Kent, Zachary. *Christopher Columbus.* Chicago: Children's Press, 1991.

McPherson, Joyce. *The River of Grace: The Story of John Calvin.* Lebanon, Tenn.: Greenleaf Press, 1998.

Sklar, Peggy A. *St. Ignatius of Loyola: In God's Service.* New York: Paulist Press, 2001.

Stepanek, Sally. *Martin Luther.* New York: Chelsea House, 1986.

Thomas, Jane Resh. *Behind the Mask: The Life of Queen Elizabeth I.* New York: Clarion, 1998.

Vernon, Louise. *The Man Who Laid the Egg: The Story of Erasmus.* Scottdale, Pa.: Herald, 1977.

———. *Bible Smuggler: The Story of William Tyndale.* Scottdale, Pa.: Herald, 1967.

AFRICA

Jordan, Manuel. *The Kongo Kingdom.* New York: Franklin Watts, 1999.

Koslow, Philip. *Mali: Crossroads of Africa.* New York: Chelsea House, 1995.

———. *Senegambia: Land of the Lion.* New York: Chelsea House, 1996.

McKissack, Patricia and Frederick. *The Royal Kingdoms of Ghana, Mail and Songhay: Life in Medieval Africa.* New York: Henry Holt, 1994.

Quigley, Mary. *Ancient West African Kingdoms: Ghana, Mali, and Songhai.* Chicago: Heinemann Library, 2002.

THE AMERICAS BEFORE COLUMBUS

Ackroyd, Peter. *Cities of Blood.* New York: DK, 2004.

Berdan, Frances. *The Aztecs.* New York: Chelsea House, 1989.

Carrasco, David. *Daily Life of the Aztecs: People of the Sun and Earth.* Westport, Conn.: Greenwood, 1998.

Editors of Time-Life Books. *Aztecs: Reign of Blood and Splendor.* Alexandria, Va.: Time-Life Books, 1992.

Fash, William, and Mary E. Lyons. *The Ancient American World.* New York: Oxford University Press, 2005.

Wood, Tim. *The Incas.* New York: Viking, 1996.

CITIES

Barter, James. *A Travel Guide to Shakespeare's London.* San Diego, Calif: Lucent, 2003.

“ *The Diary of Baron Waldstein, a Traveller in Elizabethan England.* Translated and annotated by G. W. Groos. London: Thames and Hudson, 1981.

Morley, Jacqueline. *A Renaissance Town: Florence.* New York: Peter Bedrick, 2001.

CONQUEST OF THE AMERICAS

“ León-Portilla, Miguel, ed. *The Broken Spears: The Aztec Account of the Conquest of Mexico.* Boston: Beacon, 1982.

Thomas, Hugh. *Conquest: Montezuma, Cortés, and the Fall of Old Mexico.* New York: Simon and Schuster, 1993.

Worth, Richard. *Pizarro and the Conquest of the Incas in World History.* Berkeley Heights, N.J.: Enslow, 2000.

ELIZABETHAN ENGLAND

Brimacombe, Peter. *All the Queen's Men: The World of Elizabeth I.* New York: St. Martin's, 2000.

Langley, Andrew, *Shakespeare's Theatre.* New York: Oxford University Press, 1999.

MING CHINA

DuTemple, Lesley A. *The Great Wall of China.* Minneapolis: Lerner, 2003.

Kranz, Rachel. *Across Asia by Land.* New York: Facts on File, 1991.

“ Wu Ch'eng-en. *Monkey: A Journey to the West.* Translated by David Kherdian. Boston: Shambhala, 2000.

THE OTTOMAN AND MUGHAL EMPIRES

Greenblatt, Miriam. *Suleyman the Magnificant and the Ottoman Empire.* Benchmark, 2002.

Mcdonald, Fiona. *A 16th Century Mosque.* New York: Peter Bedrick, 1994.

Rothfarb, Ed. *In the Land of the Taj Mahal: The World of the Fabled Mughals.* New York: Henry Holt, 1998.

THE PLAGUE

Dunn, John M. *Life During the Black Death.* San Diego, Calif.: Lucent, 2000.

Giblin, James Cross. *When Plague Strikes: The Black Death, Smallpox, AIDS.* New York: HarperCollins, 1995.

RENAISSANCE ART

Barter, James. *A Renaissance Painter's Studio.* San Diego, Calif.: Greenhaven, 2002.

Lassieur, Allison. *Leonardo da Vinci and the Renaissance in World History.* Berkeley Heights, N.J.: Enslow, 2000.

Mason, Antony. *In the Time of Michelangelo.* Brookfield, Conn.: Copper Beech, 2001.

THE SLAVE TRADE

Feelings, Tom. *The Middle Passage: White Ships, Black Cargo.* New York: Dial, 1995.

Haskins, James. *Bound for America: The Forced Migration of Africans to the New World.* New York: Lothrop, Lee and Shepard, 1999.

Palmer, Colin A. *The First Passage: Blacks in the Americas, 1520–1617.* New York: Oxford University Press, 1995.

TRAVELERS AND EXPLORERS

Berggren, Laurence. *Over the Edge of the World: Magellan's Terrifying Circumnavigation of the Globe.* New York: William Morrow, 2003.

Fritz. Jean. *Around the World in a Hundred Years: From Henry the Navigator to Magellan.* New York: Putnam, 1994.

Goodman, Joan Elizabeth. *A Long and Uncertain Journey: The 27,000 Mile Voyage of Vasco da Gama.* New York: Mikaya, 2001.

Hynson, Colin. *Columbus and the Renaissance Explorers.* Hauppauge, N.Y.: Barron's Educational, 2000.

———. *Magellan and the Exploration of South America.* Hauppauge, N.Y.: Barron's Educational, 1998.

Kimmel, Elizabeth Cody. *Before Columbus: The Leif Eriksson Expedition.* New York: Random House, 2003.

Levinson, Nancy Smiler. *Magellan and the First Voyage Around the World.* New York: Clarion, 2001.

Stefoff, Rebecca. *The Accidental Explorers.* New York: Oxford University Press, 1992.

Waldman, Stuart. *We Asked for Nothing: The Remarkable Journey of Cabeza de Vaca.* New York: Mikaya, 2003.

WEBSITES

GATEWAYS

English Renaissance Literature and History
www.luminarium.org/renlit/index.html
Provides links to sites on Henry VIII, Elizabeth, Shakespeare, and others, many of them multimedia.

Medieval and Modern History Sourcebooks
www.fordham.edu/halsall/sbook.html
www.fordham.edu/halsall/mod/modsbook.html
Complete texts of a huge number of original sources, compiled by Paul Halsall at Fordham University. All in the public domain and downloadable.

Women in World History
www.womeninworldhistory.com
Provides extensive links and lesson plans, including women in China, Japan, and the Islamic world. By Lyn Reese, a secondary school teacher and consultant in California.

WEBSITES

1492—An Ongoing Voyage
www.ibiblio.org/expo/1492.exhibit/Intro.html
Web-based version of an exhibit at the Library of Congress, with lots of information on the Mediterranean, Caribbean, and Americas at the time of Columbus, and on Columbus himself. Good visuals.

Age of Exploration
www.mariner.org/educationalad/ageofex/index.php
Excellent on-line curriculum of exploration from the ancient world through Captain Cook's South Sea voyages in the 18th century. From the Mariners' Museum in Newport News, Virginia.

The Atlantic Slave Trade and Slave Life in the Americas
http://hitchcock.itc.virginia.edu/Slavery/
A thousand images of the slave trade and slave life, many of them from pre-colonial Africa.

CNN Millennium
www.cnn.com/SPECIALS/1999/millennium/
Multimedia website from the CNN Millennium series, with sections on each century from the 11th through the 20th. Includes profiles, timelines, maps, and an interesting feature on artifacts. Very global in scope.

Conquistadors
www.pbs.org/opb/conquistadors/home.htm
Interactive website to accompany the PBS series on the Conquistadors. Excellent activities and resources about the Spanish and Native Americans. In English and Spanish.

Decameron Web—Plague
www.brown.edu/Departments/Italian_Studies/dweb/plague/
Texts and images of the plague, developed by the Department of Italian Studies at Brown University.

History of Timbuktu
www.timbuktufoundation.org/history.html
Story of Timbuktu and the surrounding area, with many illustrations and original sources, sponsored by the Timbuktu Educational Foundation.

Leonardo da Vinci
www.mos.org/doc/1016
Interactive virtual exhibit on Leonardo as artist and inventor, hosted by the Museum of Science, Boston.

Leonardo da Vinci
www.museoscienza.org/english/leonardo/default.htm
Virtual museum hosted by the National Museum of Science and Technology in Milan, Italy. With lots of visuals, including demonstrations of Leonardo's machines.

Martin Luther: Reluctant Revolutionary
www.pbs.org/empires/martinluther/index.html
Attractive website with many visuals, designed to go with the PBS series on Luther. Includes an interactive feature on a monk's daily life.

Ming China
www.wsu.edu:8080/~dee/MING/MING1.HTM
Section of Washington State University's World Civilizations Internet Classroom and Anthology. Provides solid information and visuals on Ming China.

Renaissance Connection
www.renaissanceconnection.org
Interactive educational website developed by the Allentown (Pennsylvania) Art Museum. Includes fun and well-researched activities on innovations, artistic patronage, and daily life.

Renaissance Culture
www.learner.org/exhibits/renaissance/
Website designed to accompany the Annenberg Foundation's Western Traditions series. With units on printing and on the city of Florence.

Renaissance Secrets
http://open2.net/renaissance2/index.html
Excellent visuals and discussion of Gutenberg and the printing press, medicine, the city of Venice, and a conspiracy against Queen Elizabeth. Presented by the BBC and the Open University in England.

INDEX

References to illustrations and their captions are indicated by page numbers in **bold**.

TEXT AND PICTURE CREDITS

TEXT CREDITS

p. 19: Christo S. Bartsocas, "Two Fourteenth-Century Descriptions of the 'Black Death,'" *Journal of the History of Medicine,* [AU: vol number?] (1966), 396, quoting John VI, *Historarum,* 395.

p. 22: Giovanni Boccaccio, *The Decameron,* trans. Mark Musa and Peter Bondanella (New York: W. W. Norton, 1982), 6–12.

p. 23: Rosemary Horrox, *The Black Death* (Manchester: Manchester University Press, 1994), 160–62.

p. 25: Ibn Battuta, *Travels in Asia and Africa, 1325–1354,* trans. and selected by H. A. R. Gibbs (New York: August M. Kelley, 1969), 69.

p. 32: Niccolò Machiavelli, *The Prince,* trans. Leo Paul S. de Alvarez (Prospect Heights, Ill.: Waveland Press, 1980), 90.

p. 35: James Bruce Ross and Mary Martin McLaughlin, eds., *The Portable Renaissance Reader* (New York: Viking, 1968), 532–38.

p. 39: Katharina Wilson, ed., *Women Writers of the Renaissance* (Athens: University of Georgia Press, 1987), 35.

p. 40: Ross and McLaughlin, eds., *The Portable Renaissance Reader,* 432.

p. 44: Kenneth J. Hammond, ed., *The Human Tradition in Premodern China* (Wilmington, Del.: Scholarly Resources, 2002), 135.

p. 46: Wing-Tsit Chan, *Chinese Philosophy,* chapter 35, cited on www.onelittelangel.com/wisdom/quotes/saint_net.asp?mc=75.

pp. 48–49: Patricia Buckley Ebrey, ed., *Chinese Civilization and Society: A Sourcebook* (New York: Free Press, 1981), 162–66.

p. 51: Hammond, ed., *The Human Tradition in Premodern China,* 163.

p. 55: Ebrey, ed., *Chinese Civilization and Society,* 141.

p. 58: Elizabeth Eisenstein, *The Printing Press as an Agent of Change: Communications and Cultural Transformations in Early Modern Europe* (Cambridge: Cambridge University Press, 1979), 72–73.

p. 63: Ibid., 342.

p. 64: John Catanzariti, ed., *The Papers of Thomas Jefferson,* vol. 28 (Princeton, N.J.: Princeton University Press, 2000), 583–84.

p. 68: Eisenstein, *The Printing Press as an Agent of Change,* 112.

p. 70: Ibid., 342.

p. 75: Harold Grimm, ed., *Luther's Works* vol. 31 (Philadelphia: Muhlenberg Press, 1957) 345, 346, 348, 359.

p. 79: G. H. Williams, ed., *Spiritual and Anabaptist Writers* (Philadelphia: Westminster, 1957), 138, 144.

p. 80: J. T. McNeill, ed., and F. L. Battles, trans., *Calvin: Institutes of the Christian Religion,* vol. 1 (Philadelphia: Westminster, 1955), 256.

p. 82: L. J. Pahl, ed., *The Spiritual Exercises of St. Ignatius* (Chicago: Loyola University Press, 1951), 1, 12.

p. 84: *The Collected Works of St. Teresa of Avila,* trans. Kieran Kavanaugh and Otilio Rodriguez, vol. 3 (Washington, D.C.: Institute of Carmelite Studies, 1976–85), 7.

p. 89: C. T. Forster and F. H. Blackburne Daniell, eds., *The Life and Letters of Ogier Ghiselin de Busbecq,* vol. 1 (London: Hakluyt Society, 1881), 155.

p. 91: Edward Peters, "Jewish History and Gentile Memory: The Expulsion of 1492," *Jewish History* 9 (1995): 23–28.

p. 94: Babur, *The* Barabur-nama *in English: Memoirs of Babur,* trans. Annette Susannah Beveridge. (London: Luzac, 1922), 124.

p. 96: *The Commentary of Father Monserrate, S.J., on His Journey to the Court of Akbar,* trans. J. S. Hoyland and S. N. Banerjee (London: Oxford University Press, 1922), 182.

p. 98: Alfred Andrea and James H Overfield, *The Human Record; Sources of Global History,* 4th ed., vol. 1 (Boston: Houghton Mifflin, 2001), 490.

p. 101: Katharina M. Wilson, *Women Writers of the Renaissance and Reformation* (Athens: University of Georgia Press, 1987), 535.

p. 103: Lisa DiCaprio and Merry E. Wiesner, eds., *Lives and Voices: Sources in European Women's History* (Boston: Houghton Mifflin, 2001), 238.

p. 107: www.timbuktufoundation.org/history.html

p. 109: *The African Past,* trans. Basil Davidson, quoted in Alfred J. Andrea and James H. Overfield, *The Human Record: Sources of Global History* (Boston, Houghton Mifflin, 2001), 473.

p. 113: Ross and McLaughlin, eds., *The Portable Renaissance Reader,* 187, 189.

p. 115: Kritovoulos, *History of Mehmed the Conqueror,* trans. Charles T. Riggs (Princeton, N.J.: Princeton University Press, 1954), 64.

p. 117: *Hernán Cortés: Letters from Mexico,* ed. and trans. A. R. Pagden (New York: Grossman, 1971), 83–84, 102, 107–8.

p. 122: James Harvey Robinson, ed. and trans., *Readings in European History,* vol. 1 (Boston: Ginn, 1904), 409–10.

p. 126: Ma Huan, *Ying-Yai Sheng-Lan: "The Overall Survey of the Ocean's Shores,"* trans. J. V. G. Mills (Cambridge: Cambridge University Press, 1970), 143.

p. 132: *Pilgrimage of Arnold von Harff, Knight...,* trans. Malcolm Letts (London: Hakluyt Society, 1946) in Ross and McLaughlin, *The Portable Renaissance Reader,* 172.

p. 134: *Travels of Marco Polo,* trans. Manuel Komroff (New York: Liveright, 1953), 312.

p. 136: Alvaro Velho, *A Journal of the First Voyage of Vasco da Gama, 1497–1499,* trans. E. G. Ravenstein. (London: Hakluyt Society, 1848), 61, 75.

p. 140: Gwyn Jones, *The Norse Atlantic Saga* (London: Oxford University Press, 1964), 146–47.

pp. 144–45: R. H. Major, ed. and trans., *Select Letters of Christopher Columbus* (London: Hakluyt Society, 1847), 1, 4, 15.

p. 147: Arthur Helps, *The Spanish Conquest in America and Its Relation to the History of Slavery and to the Government of the Colonies*, vol. 1 (London: J.W. Parker and Sons, 1855–1861), 264–67.

p. 148: C. R. Markham, ed. and trans., *The Letters of Amerigo Vespucci* (London: Hakluyt Society, 1894), 28.

p. 159: *China in the Sixteenth Century: The Journals of Matteo Ricci*, trans. Louis J. Gallagher, (New York: Random House, 1942), 216.

p. 161: Michael Cooper, ed., *They Came to Japan: An Anthology of European Reports on Japan, 1543–1640* (Berkeley: University of California Press, 1965), 40.

p. 162: Richard Ligon, *True and Exact History of the Island of Barbadoes* (London: Parker and Guy, 1673), n.p.

p. 164: Edwin Reynolds, *Stand the Storm: A History of the Atlantic Slave Trade* (London: Allison and Busby, 1985), 45.

p. 168: *The Codex Mendoza*, trans. Frances F. Berdan and Patricia Rieff Anawalt, vol. 4 (Berkeley: University of California Press, 1992), 34–35.

pp. 170–71: Miguel Leon-Portilla, ed., *The Broken Spears: The Aztec Account of the Conquest of Mexico* (Boston: Beacon, 1982), 63, 67, 93.

p. 177: Huamán Poma, *Letter to a King: A Peruvian Chief's Account of Life under the Incas and under Spanish Rule*, ed. Christopher Dilke (New York: Dutton, 1978), 135.

p. 181: Kenneth Mills and William B. Taylor, eds., *Colonial Spanish America: A Documentary History* (Wilmington, Del.: Scholarly Resources, 1998), 174.

PICTURE CREDITS

Art Resource, NY: 32; Bibliothèque Nationale de France: 16; Photo by Author: 118, 121; Bildarchiv Preussischer Kulturbesitz / Art Resource, NY: 57, 76, 151, 154, 161, 172, 173; Bodleian Library, University of Oxford: 131; Borromeo / Art Resource, NY: 91; Bridgeman-Giraudon / Art Resource, NY: 64, 85, 88, 127, 158; By Permission of the British Library Ms. Add. 1039: 92; By Permission of the British Library Or.8210/P.2: Cover, 59; By Permission of the British Library Royal 2 A.XVI f.63v: 98; © The Trustees of the British Museum: 50, 114, 125; Courtesy of the John Carter Brown Library at Brown University: 107; Cameraphoto Arte, Venice / Art Resource, NY: 69; © The trustees of the Chester Beatty Library, Dublin: 130; *Trionfo d'amore*, Petrarch, 4648, Bd ms 32 (early 16th century), Courtesy of the Division of Rare and Manuscript Collections, Cornell University Library: 38; Erich Lessing / Art Resource, NY: 12, 26, 30, 36, 48, 55, 117, 160; By Permission of the Folger Shakespeare Library: 101; Foto Marburg / Art Resource, NY: 31, 67; © Germanisches National Museum: 75; Courtesy of the Harvard-Yenching Library, Harvard University, from the 1833 Bunsei edition of *Journey to the West*: 53; HIP / Art Resource, NY: 14, 100, 109, 133; Image Select / Art Resource, NY: 24; Courtesy of Society of Kunqu Arts, Inc., Potomac, Md, "The Peony Pavilion" 12/14/03 performance (Grace Hui-hsin Wang, left, Margaret Xu, right): 41; Library of Congress, Prints and Photographs Division: 84; Library of Congress, Geography and Map Division: 138, 148; Library of Congress, Rare Book and Special Collections: 141, 155; The Mariners' Museum, Newport News, VA: 52, 140, 146, 150; All Rights Reserved, The Metropolitan Museum of Art, Harris Brisbane Dick Fund, 1927 (27.5.2.). Photograph, all rights reserved, The Metropolitan Museum of Art: 35; The Metropolitan Museum of Art, Edward Elliot Family Collection, Gift of Douglas Dillion, 1986 (1986.266.3) Photograph © 1981 The Metropolitan Museum of Art: 52; The Metropolitan Museum of Art, Gift of Robert E. Tod, 1937 (37.191.1) Photograph © 1986 The Metropolitan Museum of Art: 51; The Metropolitan Museum of Art, Purchase, Florence and Herbert Irving Gift, 1992 (1992.131) Photograph © 1993 The Metropolitan Museum of Art: 93; The Metropolitan Museum of Art, Purchase, The Dillion Fund Gift, 1989 (1989.141.3) Photograph © 1995 The Metropolitan Museum of Art: 45; The Metropolitan Museum of Art, Seymour Fund, 1959 (59.49.1) Photograph © 2002 The Metropolitan Museum of Art: 47; The Metropolitan Museum of Art, The Michael C. Rockefeller Memorial Collection, Bequest of Nelson A. Rockefeller 1979 (1979.206.116) Photograph © 1981 The Metropolitan Museum of Art: 105; Title woodcut from Bartholomaeus Metlinger, Regiment der jungen Kinder (Augsburg: Guenther Zainer, 1473): 119; The Pierpont Morgan Library / Art Resource, NY: 39, 63, 72, 142, 174, 178; © Musée National de la Marine: 13 (bottom); © National Maritime Museum: 13(top), 135, 153; General Research Division, The New York Public Library, Astor, Lenox and Tilden Foundations: 164; New York Public Library / Art Resource, NY: 110, 147, 162; © Osterreichische Nationalbibliothek, Vienna, Cod. 8. 626.f.63: 90; Detail of Shen Tu's The Tribute Giraffe with Attendant, Philadelphia Museum of Art, Gift of John T. Dorrance, 1977: 123; Dols, Michael W., *The Black Death In The Middle Ages* © 1977 Princeton University Press, 2005 renewed PUP. Reprinted by permission of the Princeton University Press: 23; Harry Ransom Humanities Research Center, The University of Texas at Austin. © Dale Guild Type Foundry: 54; The Royal Collection © 2004, Her Majesty Queen Elizabeth II: 97; Royal Geographical Society, London: 122; Réunion des Musées Nationaux/Art Resource, NY: 43, 80, 113; David Day Photographer, Courtesy of Columbus Santa Maria, Inc. The Santa Maria, Columbus, OH: 139; Scala / Art Resource, NY: 18, 27, 28, 34, 65, 71, 73, 11,176; Schalkwijk/ Art Resource, NY: 116, 165; Science Museum / Science & Society Picture Library: 22; SEF / Art Resource, NY: cover, 56; Snark / Art Resource, NY: 19, 33, 78, 81, 83, 136, 169; Johann Amos Commenii *Orbis Sensualium Pictus*... by Charles Hoole, London 16[59]? pp.190–91, University College Dublin Library: 60; University Library, Utrecht, Ms 842, fol. 132r: 40; Vanni / Art Resource, NY: 96; Victoria and Albert Museum, London / Art Resource, NY: 94, 95, 103; Werner Forman / Art Resource, NY: 2, 20, 104, 128, 134, 137, 152, 156, 167, 171, 177.

ACKNOWLEDGMENTS

My thanks to my friends and colleagues Ellen Amster, Martha Carlin, Jean Fleet, Jay Harmon, Scott Hendrix, David Whitford, and Ying Wang for their help and suggestions.

MERRY E. WIESNER-HANKS is professor of history and director of the Center for Women's Studies at the University of Wisconsin-Milwaukee. She is one of the authors of *Discovering the Global Past, Discovering the Western Past* and several other titles in a series of innovative books that give students the opportunity to *do* history the same way historians do—examining original sources to answer questions about the past. Professor Wiesner-Hanks is also the coeditor of the *Sixteenth Century Journal* and the author or editor of 12 other books and many articles, written in English and German, about the lives of women and men around the world, especially in the 14th through the 18th centuries. These include specialized studies of women's work, the role of Christianity in family life, the Protestant Reformation, citizenship, and servants. Her research, for which she has been awarded Fulbright and Guggenheim Fellowships, has been translated into Spanish, Italian, and Chinese.

BONNIE G. SMITH is Board of Governors Professor of History at Rutgers University. She has edited a series for teachers on Women's and Gender History in Global Perspective for the American Historical Association and has served as chair of the test development committee for the Advanced Placement examination in European history. Professor Smith is the author of many books on European, comparative, and women's history, among them *Confessions of a Concierge* and *Imperialism: A History in Documents.* She is co-author of *The Making of the West: Peoples and Cultures,* editor in chief of the forthcoming Oxford encyclopedia on women in world history, and general editor of an Oxford world history series for high school students and general readers.

Morgan